COMPLETE STUDY GUIDE

Securities Representatives' Examinations

For BROKERS, STOCK and BOND SALESMEN, MUTUAL FUND REPRESENTATIVES

By Frank Stefano, Jr.
National Training Director, Hornblower & Weeks-Hemphill, Noyes

arco
219 Park Avenue South, New York, N.Y. 10003

Published by ARCO PUBLISHING COMPANY, Inc.
219 Park Avenue South, New York, N.Y. 10003

Library of Congress Catalog Card Number 78-77260
Arco Catalog Number: SBN 668-01934-4
Manufactured in the United States of America

FOREWORD

These 500 questions cover all major topics mentioned in the New York Stock Exchange "Study Outline for Registration Examinations" for candidates for full, or standard examination for registered representatives with a New York Stock Exchange Member Firm.

The questions are meant to be used as a review at the conclusion of extensive study and preparation. In no way should they be considered sufficient preparation in and of themselves to meet the high qualification examination standards of the New York Stock Exchange.

This booklet is also worthwhile for the candidate for NASD only examination requirements. In that case, ignore the last 50 questions in Part 1.

The questions are hopefully worded in such a way as to illustrate principals or concepts on a particular point and to provide amplification and clarification of the knowledge of the trainee. In addition, each of the answers shows a reference or rule number, in parentheses after the correct answer choice, that identifies the reference source where information relating to the question and the correct answer may be found. For example, the reference for question 1, part 1, 1. C (7); the seventh book in the List of References is The Stock Market, Leffler, Farwell.

There are 75 questions on each major topic area of the NYSE Study Outline, plus an additional 50 questions on the NYSE. All questions are in the same multiple choice format as used on all NASD and NYSE examinations for registered representatives. The questions are assembled in the same outline order as provided in the New York Stock Exchange Study Outline.

CONTENTS

STUDY OUTLINE FOR REGISTRATION EXAMINATIONS*

The New York Stock Exchange requires registration of all employees of member firms engaged in the solicitation or handling of securities business. The Exchange believes that all such employees should have a common body of general knowledge concerning securities, their issuers, their marketing, and business practices of the industry. Consequently, there is but one class of full registration, permitting each representative to offer the full range of investment service, even though he may specialize in a particular area. Exchange examinations, taken at the conclusion of the required training and experience period, reflect in their subject balance the necessity for a broad competence in all phases of the securities business.

The New York Stock Exchange and the National Association of Securities Dealers conduct a simplified examination program for the candidates for registration with both organizations, permitting candidates to satisfy the examination requirements of both the NYSE and the NASD at one test session rather than at two sessions. Coordination of examinations is as follows:

STANDARD EXAMINATION — The work of most registered representatives demands a depth knowledge of corporate securities, especially stocks. The Standard Examination for full registration, through which all but a very few candidates qualify, is designed to meet this demand. As the outline in the following pages indicates, the Standard Examination tests on a broad range of securities knowledge, and in depth on corporate stocks.

Under the coordinated examination program, the Exchange accepts the 125 question NASD Examination in partial fulfillment of its own examination requirement. The NASD Examination consists of 100 General Securities Knowledge questions and 25 questions on the NASD. To these, the Exchange adds a 50 question NYSE Section covering round and odd-lot trading, Exchange Constitution and Rules, and the more difficult aspects of corporate finance and security analysis. Candidates are scored on their answers to the combined total of 175 questions.

The coordination of NYSE and NASD examinations is a procedural simplification for candidates of NYSE member firms. It is not a combination of registration requirements, which must still be met separately for both organizations.

Requirements for registration with the states, which in many cases include an examination on securities laws of individual states, must also be met separately.

The Exchange's examinations contain equally

weighted multiple-choice questions. These consist of a stem and four optional answers, of which one is correct or best. Although they require careful and precise reading, they are not designed to be "tricky". Candidates who are well prepared on the subject of a question will immediately see the correct or best answer. The less desirable or incorrect answers, however, are written in such a way that they seem plausible to the poorly prepared candidate, and he consequently may think them "tricky".

Here is an example of this type of question:

Short term credits are normally secured through

1. bonds.
2. deeds of trust.
3. notes.
4. mortgages.

The correct answer is the third, but readers who are not well acquainted with the subject may have picked one of the three incorrect answers.

The Exchange examinations, being entirely objective in form, are graded by machine with no possibility of bias or interpretation by a grader. Each examination form is of comparable difficulty based on actual pre-testing of the questions with large numbers of candidates. Grades are reported to member firms on the following scale:

A, superior — top 10% of all candidates

B, above average — 65th to 90th percentile of all candidates

C, average — 35th to 65th percentile

D, below average — under the 35th percentile

F, failure

Letter grades are revised quarterly based on candidate's performance, except for the passing score which is established independently.

The following outline is designed to indicate the subject coverage and subject balance of the Standard Examination for full registration. It is not possible to list separately each point on which candidates are subject to examination. Therefore, in using the outline for guidance and review, candidates should interpret each topic mentioned to include details which, though unspecified, could reasonably be expected to pertain.

I ELEMENTS OF FINANCE

A. Corporation Finance and Accounting

1. The corporation — Legal status, state charter, stockholders, directors, officers. Rights and liabilities of stockholders, voting, proxies, cumulative voting, pre-emptive right.

2. Ownership securities — Common stock, rights, warrants, splits, par value. Preferred stock, cumulative, participating and convertible features. Authorized, outstanding, unissued and treasury stock. Cash and stock dividends.

3. Debt securities — Debentures, mortgage bonds, equipment and collateral trust certificates, income bonds. Retirement, convertible, serial and sinking fund bonds. Interest, coupons.

4. Corporate accounting — Basics of double entry bookkeeping, balance sheet and profit and loss statement. Current and fixed assets, current and long term liabilities, capital and surplus, asset value, book value. Depreciation, depletion, amortization, LIFO and FIFO costing methods.

B. Municipal Securities

1. Municipal bonds — general obligation bonds, tax anticipation notes, guaranteed bonds. Total and floating debt. Full faith and credit of issuer.
2. Revenue bonds — Type and legal status of issuer, statutory authorities. New Housing Authority bonds, special tax and assessment bonds. Balloon maturities.
3. State bonds.

C. Foreign securities

1. Special characteristics and risks, expropriation, currency conversion, different accounting and disclosure, par value system of trading and dividends.
2. American depositary receipts.

D. U. S. Government Securities and the Money Market

1. Types of U. S. securities — treasury bills, tax anticipation bills, certificates of indebtedness, notes, bonds. Maturities and methods of interest payment for each.

2. The money market — types of instruments traded, methods of trading, sources of funds, money market indicators. Importance of Federal Funds. Interpretation of the Weekly Condition Statement. Interest rates.

3. Treasury and Federal Board Controls, debt and fiscal management. Federal Reserve functions, open market operations, discount window, reserve requirements, moral suasion.

E. Taxation

1. Personal income tax — progressive rates, short and long term capital gains, capital losses, carry-forward of losses. Dividend income credit and exclusion. Tax free status of municipal securities.

2. Inheritance tax — valuation of securities in estate, cost accepted for tax purposes; gift tax — annual and lifetime.

3. Corporate income taxes, excise and other taxes.

4. Interest Equalization Tax.

F. Economic Trends

1. Broad factors affecting securities and securities markets — inflation and deflation, government and private spending, growth and movement of population, international gold and currency flow.

2. Economic forecasters, indices, GNP.

II ANALYSIS OF SECURITIES

A. Evaluation of Corporate Securities

1. Financial statements — appraisal of profitability, growth, stability, liquidity. Balance sheet, current ratio, net quick ratio, debt equity ratio, leverage. Profit and loss statement, inventory and depreciation policy, cash flow, inventory turnover, net profit relation to capitalization. Effect of merger, consolidation, refinancing, recapitalization, reorganization, receivership.

2. Common Stock — Price earnings ratio, dividend payout, yield, relation of book value to market price. Blue chip, growth and speculative stocks, special situations. Effect of stock splits and dividends, valuation of rights.

3. Corporate Senior Securities — Coverage for preferred stock dividends and bond interest, calculation of overall coverage. Appraisal of callable and conversion provisions, prémium and discount, yield to maturity. Trust Indenture Act of 1939.

4. Industry Analysis — Major classifications of industries and characteristics of each, effect of major economic and social changes on each. Standards used to measure company performance within industry classifications.

5. Market Analysis — Technical approach as contrasted with fundamental approach. Stock indexes and averages, trading volume, short interest. Odd-lot theory, Dow theory, chart interpretation, resistance zones, support levels.

B. Evaluation of Municipal and U. S. Government Securities

1. Analysis of municipal or state unit, willingness and ability to pay, default record, legal borrowing limit, debt trend, ratio of debt to assessed valuation, per capita debt, ratio of debt service to total revenues. Analysis of authority issuing revenue bonds, earning power, coverage, application of corporate analytical standards.

2. Analysis of U. S. Government securities — matching of maturities, estate tax features.

C. Portfolio Analysis

1. Tailoring investment programs to specific individual and institutional needs. Preservation of capital, growth, income.

2. Planning investment programs — family

situations, income and inheritance tax considerations, emergency provisions, life insurance coverage, capacity to accept risk.

3. Formula investing — dollar cost averaging, constant ratio and constant dollar plans, trend following, scale trading.

III INVESTMENT COMPANIES

A. Fundamentals of investment companies

1. Distinction between closed-end including dual purpose funds and open-end companies (mutual funds), capitalization of each.
2. Types of open-end investment companies, diversified common stock, specialized by industry or geography, preferred stock and bond, and characteristics of each. Objectives and policies — growth, income, and balanced funds. Fully managed funds. Specialized funds for narrowly limited purposes.
3. Operation of investment companies — operating costs, management fees, expense ratio, sales charge, custodian charge, net investment income, unrealized appreciation, dividend and capital gains distribution.
4. Taxation of mutual fund shareowners — passing through of taxation of dividends and capital gains, required dividend payout and capital gains distribution under Internal Revenue Code.
5. Prospectus and Annual Report — applicable provisions of Securities Act of 1933.

B. Investment Company Act of 1940

1. Definitions and provisions of the act, "regulated investment company," maintaining public offering price.

C. Marketing Open-End Investment Company Shares

1. Methods of issue and redemption, basis for bid and asked prices, changing number of shares outstanding, calculation of net asset value per share. Quantity discount, letter of intent, automatic dividend reinvestment, conditional sales, breakpoint sales.
2. Accumulation plans — level charge, open account. Prepaid charge (contractual) plan, penalty for discontinuance in early years. Plan completion insurance.
3. Withdrawal plans — possible reduction of principal amount through sale of shares.
4. SEC Statement of Policy — applicability to oral as well as written presentations, list of materially misleading acts in sale of investment company shares, performance charts and tables. Delegation of authority to NASD in enforcement.

IV SECURITIES BUSINESS PROCEDURES

A. Agency and Principal Functions and Responsibilities

1. Moral and legal obligations of the registered representative, law of agency, disclosure of control or participation, disclosure of broker or dealer position.
2. Securities firm organization, operations, sales, research. Corporate affiliates and guaranteed corporate subsidiaries.
3. SEC rules — registration and capital requirements for broker-dealers.

B. Handling of Accounts

1. Procedures and necessary papers for opening and closing of accounts, joint accounts, discretionary accounts, corporate accounts, investment clubs.
2. Handling orders and keeping records, organization of customer information.
3. Forwarding of proxy material to beneficial owners.

C. Securities Transactions

1. Kinds of orders and their uses — round and odd-lot, limited, stop, long, short, ex-dividend, discretionary, for "cash," regular way, delayed delivery, seller's option.
2. Commissions, Federal and state taxes.
3. Clearing, settlement and delivery, clearing houses, transfer methods, marking to the

market. Record date, "when, as, and if" issued. Endorsement of certificates for good delivery, handling of street name certificates, due bills. Registration of stock, delivery.

4. Credit — provisions of Regulation T and Regulation U, NYSE initial and maintenance margin rules, extensions granted by NYSE and NASD, interest, prompt payment. Segregation and hypothecation of customer securities.

D. State Law

1. Blue sky laws, definition of "domestic" and "foreign" securities. Legal investments, prudent man rule, gifts of securities to minors under Uniform Acts.

V ORGANIZED EXCHANGES

A. New York Stock Exchange Operations

1. Functions, historical background, functions of Board of Governors and staff. Five types of Floor activity by members.
2. Round lot market — the specialist system, parity, priority and precedence, crossing, stopping, matching, errors, stock ahead, delivery dates. Arbitrage. Bond trading.
3. Odd-lot system — the odd-lot houses as dealers, effective sale, differentials, execution of odd-lot orders, "basis" price.
4. Short selling — 1934 Act provisions, minus or zero-minus tick. Danger in thin markets.
5. Ticker and quotations — reading and interpreting the tape or other electronic devices, reading newspaper stock tables.
6. Block handling — procedures for handling blocks of listed stock.
7. Monthly Investment Plan — eligible stocks, features, procedures.
8. Listing of stocks — listing and delisting standards, disclosure, proxy requirements.
9. Stock Clearing Corp, Central Certificate Service.
10. Securities Exchange Act of 1934 — prohibited abuses (Sec. 9A and 10B), registration of broker/dealers (15A), manipulation and fraud (15), unlawful representations (26).

B. New York Stock Exchange Constitution and Rules

1. Objects of Exchange as expressed in the Constitution, unwritten interpretation that rules governing members and member firms extend to registered representatives. Arbitration.
2. Registered representatives — standards for registration, training, investigation, examination, Registered Representative Agreements. Full time employment. Limit of credit on own account, gratuities to employees or other non-members.
3. Conduct of accounts — due diligence to learn essential facts, "know your customer." Designation of accounts, occupational restrictions, discretionary accounts, statements to customers.
4. NYSE rules to safeguard firm solvency and protect customers from firm loss. Capital rules, audits, examinations, financial statements, financial questionnaires, underwriting reports.
5. Advertising — standards for NYSE approval, application to oral presentations.

C. Other Exchanges

1. American Stock Exchange — functions and history.
2. Regional exchanges — dual listing of NYSE stocks.
3. Foreign exchanges — methods of listing and trading.

VI OVER-THE-COUNTER MARKETS AND THE NASD

A. Fundamentals

1. Characteristics — negotiation rather than auction, broker and deal functions.

2. Securities traded — corporate stocks and bonds, municipal bonds, U. S. Government securities.

B. Trading

1. Operation of over-the-counter markets, telephone communications, dealer positions.
2. Role of the over-the-counter trader, terms and expressions used in trading.
3. Quotations — Bid and asked, spread, pink sheets.
4. Security Options — puts and calls.

C. Investment Banking

1. Functions of the investment banker — underwriting and selling, primary and secondary distributions.
2. Investment banking procedures — syndicate, "due diligence" meeting, competitive bidding, negotiation, "best efforts," private placement, selling, group, stabilization.
3. Applicable law — Securities Act of 1933, registration, "red herring," indication of interest, prospectus, exemptions.

D. The National Association of Securities Dealers

1. Background and purposes — Certificate of Incorporation and By-Laws.
2. Rules of Fair Practice — recommendations to customers, charges, fair prices and commissions, publication of purchases and sales, nominal quotations, offers at stated prices, disclosure of price and concessions, securities taken in trade, use of fiduciary information, rewarding others' employees, paying to influence market prices. Disclosure of dealer or broker position, control, participation or interest. Discretionary accounts. Office of Supervisory Jurisdiction.
3. Uniform Practice Code — purposes and provisions.
4. Interpretations — 5% policy, advertising, free riding and withholding, enforcement of SEC rules pertaining to sale of open-end investment company shares.
5. Code of Procedure — purposes.
6. Resolutions of the Board of Governors — purposes and scope.

LIST OF REFERENCES

1. *New York Stock Exchange Constitution & Rules,* New York Stock Exchange, New York, N. Y.

2. *NASD Manual,* National Association of Securities Dealers, Washington, D. C.

3. *NASD Training Guide,* National Association of Securities Dealers, Washington, D. C.

4. *Fundamentals of the Money Market,* New York Stock Exchange, New York, N. Y.

5. *How to Invest on a Budget — MIP (Monthly Investment Plan),* New York Stock Exchange, New York, N. Y.

6. *The Interpretation of Financial Statements,* Graham & McGolrick — Harper & Row, Publishers, New York, N. Y.

7. *The Stock Market,* Leffler, Farwell — Ronald Press Company, New York, N. Y.

8. *Securities* — Volume 2, Second Edition; *Financial Planning and Mutual Funds,* Kalb, Voorhis & Co., New York, N. Y.

9. *Your Federal Income Tax,* Internal Revenue Service — Production Company, Scarborough, New York.

10. *Manual for Registered Representatives,* Association of Stock Exchange Firms (ASEF), New York, N. Y.

11. *American Stock Exchange Constitution,* American Stock Exchange, New York, N. Y.

ARCO PRACTICE ANSWER SHEET

1. Elements of Finance

USE THE SPECIAL PENCIL. MAKE GLOSSY BLACK MARKS.

1 A B C D
2 A B C D
3 A B C D
4 A B C D
5 A B C D
6 A B C D
7 A B C D
8 A B C D
9 A B C D
10 A B C D
11 A B C D
12 A B C D
13 A B C D
14 A B C D
15 A B C D
16 A B C D
17 A B C D
18 A B C D
19 A B C D
20 A B C D
21 A B C D
22 A B C D
23 A B C D
24 A B C D
25 A B C D
26 A B C D
27 A B C D
28 A B C D
29 A B C D
30 A B C D
31 A B C D
32 A B C D
33 A B C D
34 A B C D
35 A B C D
36 A B C D
37 A B C D
38 A B C D
39 A B C D
40 A B C D
41 A B C D
42 A B C D
43 A B C D
44 A B C D
45 A B C D
46 A B C D
47 A B C D
48 A B C D
49 A B C D
50 A B C D
51 A B C D
52 A B C D
53 A B C D
54 A B C D
55 A B C D
56 A B C D
57 A B C D
58 A B C D
59 A B C D
60 A B C D
61 A B C D
62 A B C D
63 A B C D
64 A B C D
65 A B C D
66 A B C D
67 A B C D
68 A B C D
69 A B C D
70 A B C D
71 A B C D
72 A B C D
73 A B C D
74 A B C D
75 A B C D

1. Elements of Finance

1. A corporation undertakes action in
   - (A) the name of its officers
   - (B) the name of its directors
   - (C) its own name
   - (D) the name of its shareholders

2. Corporations are granted charters by
   - (A) a particular state
   - (B) the Securities and Exchange Commission
   - (C) the New York Stock Exchange
   - (D) their shareholders

3. A corporation is owned by its
   - (A) stockholders
   - (B) officers
   - (C) directors
   - (D) bondholders

4. All of the following are considered advantages of the corporate form of business entity *except*:
   - (A) unlimited life
   - (B) unlimited liability
   - (C) ease of raising capital
   - (D) tax rates contrasted to individual tax rates

5. Directors of a corporation are
   - (A) elected by the shareholders
   - (B) elected by the officers of the corporation
   - (C) appointed by the officers of the corporation
   - (D) appointed by the New York Stock Exchange

6. A shareholder of a corporation has the right to
   - (A) receipt of dividends, when declared
   - (B) elect officers of the company
   - (C) inspect the accounting books of the company
   - (D) receive information on the company before it is released to the general public and the press

7. A proxy is a power of attorney granted by the
   - (A) shareholder to authorize another to vote his stock
   - (B) corporation to authorize another to vote its stock
   - (C) shareholder to authorize another to vote his debt securities
   - (D) corporation to authorize another to vote its debt securities

8. A shareholder may change his vote
   - (A) even after granting a proxy to another
   - (B) only before granting a proxy to another
   - (C) in no case once he signs a proxy
   - (D) only by appearing at the company meeting and voting in person

9. The two classifications of corporate voting are:
   - (A) preferred and cumulative
   - (B) cumulative and preferred
   - (C) ownership and statutory
   - (D) cumulative and statutory

10. The major characteristic of statutory voting is
    (A) one vote per share owned for each director
    (B) one vote per share owned for each officer
    (C) multiplying the number of shares owned by the number of officers to be elected
    (D) multiplying the number of shares owned by the number of directors to be elected

11. The pre-emptive right permits the
    (A) common shareholder to maintain his proportionate share of ownership in the corporation
    (B) preferred shareholder to maintain his proportionate share of ownership in the corporation
    (C) holder of debt securities to maintain his proportionate share in the corporation
    (D) corporation to maintain its share of the industry by issuing additional securities

12. Ownership securities include all of the following *except*:
    (A) debentures
    (B) common stock
    (C) preferred stock
    (D) warrants

13. Securities which evidence ownership are known as
    (A) guaranteed securities
    (B) debt securities
    (C) equity securities
    (D) government securities

14. If a shareholder does not exercise a stock right his proportionate interest in that issue is
    (A) reduced
    (B) increased
    (C) unchanged
    (D) unable to be determined from this information

15. A stock warrant gives the holder the right to purchase a security
    (A) at a stated price within a specified period of time
    (B) at a stated price on a specified date in the future
    (C) within a stated range of prices for a specified period of time
    (D) within a stated range of price on a specified date in the future

16. Typically the marketability of the shares of a stock that has split are
    (A) unchanged
    (B) decreased
    (C) increased in direct percent to the split
    (D) improved

17. Par value for common stock
    (A) is the price at which the corporation will redeem the stock
    (B) is always directly related to the market price of the stock
    (C) has no relation to market price of the common stock
    (D) is the stock's liquidation value

18. The receipt of a specified dividend before payments are made to common shareholders is a right of
    (A) preferred stockholders
    (B) warrant owners
    (C) debenture owners
    (D) mortgage bondholders

19. Preferred stock is a form of
    (A) debt
    (B) equity ownership
    (C) debt structure of the corporation
    (D) full unrestricted ownership of the corporation

20. Cumulative preferred shareholders
    (A) receive the stated dividend plus a share in the earnings available for the common stock
    (B) have a claim to the stated dividend whether or not earned or declared

(C) may convert, under certain conditions, their shares into common stock
(D) have the right to retire the shares at a specified price

21. The authorized stock of a corporation is the number of shares

(A) permitted to be distributed by the corporation's charter
(B) in the hands of the public
(C) issued, less Treasury stock
(D) issued, plus Treasury stock

22. Treasury stock

(A) has no vote nor are dividends paid on it
(B) has no vote, but dividends are paid
(C) can be voted, but no dividends are paid on it
(D) can be voted and does receive dividends

23. Dividends may be declared and paid on

(A) collateral trust certificates
(B) debentures
(C) equipment trust certificates
(D) common stock

24. Typically dividends are paid

(A) semi-annually
(B) monthly
(C) quarterly
(D) annually

25. When a corporation pays a dividend in property, it usually is in the form of

(A) stock of another corporation
(B) fixed assets of another corporation
(C) fixed assets of the corporation issuing the dividend
(D) a reverse stock split

26. Debentures are backed by

(A) the general credit standing of the issuing corporation
(B) specific pledge of heavy equipment
(C) specific pledge of real property
(D) specific pledge of stocks or bonds of another corporation

27. Mortgage bonds which have prior claim over all other mortgages are

(A) consolidated mortgage bonds
(B) second mortgage bonds
(C) general mortgage bonds
(D) first mortgage bonds

28. Equipment trust certificates are usually issued by

(A) utilities
(B) railroad companies
(C) shipping companies
(D) steel companies

29. Another name for income bonds is

(A) adjustment bonds
(B) revenue bonds
(C) general obligations
(D) debentures

30. Income bonds, being a debt security, pay interest

(A) only when and if earned
(B) every quarter
(C) every six months
(D) once a year

31. A bond issue can be redeemed

(A) by any of the following methods
(B) through conversion privileges
(C) through retirement
(D) by refinancing of another issue

32. An issue of bonds which would have different maturity dates is a

(A) Convertible Bond
(B) Sinking Fund Bond
(C) Serial Bond
(D) Debenture

33. Normally bonds are issued in denominations of

(A) $100
(B) $5,000
(C) $10,000
(D) $1,000

34. The financial statement which shows a corporation's status as of a specific point of time is the

(A) balance sheet
(B) profit and loss statement
(C) income statement
(D) registration statement

35. The balance sheet

(A) reports expenses and costs
(B) shows what the company owns and owes
(C) indicates net profit or loss for that year
(D) reports earnings retained in the business

36. Examples of current assets are

(A) tools and equipment
(B) land and buildings
(C) accounts receivable and inventories
(D) accounts and notes payable

37. An example of a deferred charge is

(A) accounts receivable
(B) wages owed
(C) a brand name or a patent
(D) pre-paid rent

38. Another name for capital and surplus is

(A) shareowner equity
(B) liabilities
(C) profit and loss statement
(D) assets

39. The book value of a stock is

(A) the value of assets applicable to that issue of stock after deducting all liabilities as well as intangible assets
(B) the market price of the stock divided by the earnings per share
(C) the market price of the stock multiplied by the earnings per share
(D) the liquidation value of the issue

40. The term depreciation is properly applied to

(A) land
(B) buildings
(C) natural resources
(D) brand names or patents

41. The term depletion is properly applied to

(A) natural resources
(B) land
(C) buildings
(D) brand names or patents

42. Amortization is defined as the writing oft over a period of time of

(A) current liabilities
(B) current assets
(C) fixed assets
(D) net worth

43. A company with large inventories of similar items would most properly use

(A) FIFO to value its inventory
(B) LIFO to value its inventory
(C) the average cost to value its inventory
(D) the average market price to value its inventory

44. The inventory evaluation which minimizes taxable profits based merely on inventory appreciation in periods of rising prices is

(A) market cost method
(B) FIFO
(C) average cost method
(D) LIFO

45. All of the following appear on a Profit and Loss Statement *except*:

(A) working capital
(B) operating expenses
(C) net income
(D) earnings per share

46. A municipal bond could be issued by any of the following *except*:

(A) a turnpike authority
(B) a sovereign state
(C) a public utility company
(D) a county school district

47. So called general obligation municipal bonds are backed by

    (A) the full faith and credit of the issuer
    (B) the revenue of the project financed
    (C) the federal government
    (D) the investment banker who underwrites the issue

48. The term "floating debt" refers to the

    (A) amount of the particular bond issue on the market at a point in time
    (B) total amount of debt securities a municipality has issued
    (C) process of underwriting a debt type obligation
    (D) dilution (watering) of an issue by increasing the size of the debt issue

49. Which of the following would be classified as a revenue bond?

    (A) New Jersey Turnpike 3¼% of '79
    (B) New Jersey State 4¾% of '75
    (C) New Jersey Telephone Debentures 4¼% of '80
    (D) Camden New Jersey School District 4% of '83

50. The interest on revenue bonds is paid from

    (A) income of the project built
    (B) taxes of the state concerned
    (C) taxes of the county or city concerned
    (D) either the income of the project or through assessments on taxpayers

51. ADR's are used to facilitate trading in

    (A) stock rights
    (B) commodities
    (C) warrants
    (D) foreign securities

52. U. S. Government Securities include

    (A) treasury bills
    (B) municipal bonds
    (C) revenue bonds
    (D) general obligation bonds

53. Treasury bills are initially sold at

    (A) par
    (B) a discount
    (C) a specific rate of interest
    (D) a premium

54. Treasury bills are

    (A) short term obligations of the money market
    (B) long term obligations of the money market
    (C) long term obligations of the capital market
    (D) short term obligations of the capital market

55. U. S. government securities that mature in 1 to 5 years from issue date are called

    (A) bonds
    (B) notes
    (C) certificates
    (D) bills

56. All of the following are instruments traded in the money market *except*:

    (A) bankers acceptances
    (B) treasury bills
    (C) commercial paper
    (D) revenue bonds

57. The Federal Reserve System

    (A) is our central bank
    (B) authorizes the issuance of money in the U. S.
    (C) prints the money used in the U. S.
    (D) issues U. S. government securities

58. The most effective tool available to the Federal Reserve System to execute and enforce its policies is its

    (A) use of the discount window
    (B) changing reserve requirements
    (C) open market operations
    (D) changing margin requirements

59. The least effective tool available to the Federal Reserve System over the money supply is through

(A) changing margin requirements
(B) open market operations
(C) reserve requirements
(D) moral suasion

60. When the Federal Reserve System buys government securities, it

(A) has no effect on the money supply
(B) decreases the money supply
(C) increases the money supply
(D) may increase or decrease the money supply depending on who buys the securities

61. Short term capital gains are taxed at

(A) ordinary income rates
(B) one half of ordinary income rates
(C) one quarter of ordinary income rates
(D) a maximum of 25% of ordinary income rates

62. In order to qualify for long term capital gain tax treatment a security must be held a minimum of

(A) six months and one day from trade date
(B) six months and one day from settlement date
(C) exactly six months from trade date
(D) under six months from trade date

63. The maximum resultant net capital loss that can be deducted annually from a joint account is

(A) $5,000
(B) $2,000
(C) $1,000
(D) the amount of the loss

64. In computing capital gains for tax purposes, which must be done first?

(A) short term gains netted against short term losses
(B) short term gains netted against long term losses
(C) short term gains added to long term gains
(D) short term losses added to long term losses

65. The IRS permits resultant net capital losses to be carried forward

(A) a maximum of 10 years
(B) a maximum of 2 years
(C) a maximum of 5 years
(D) indefinitely

66. Current IRS tax provisions permit the exclusion of

(A) the first $50 of all dividends received from qualifying corporations
(B) 4% of all dividends received from qualifying corporations
(C) 5% of all dividends received from qualifying corporations
(D) the first $100 received in dividends from qualifying corporations

67. Interest from municipal securities is always tax free from

(A) federal income taxes
(B) state income taxes
(C) city income taxes
(D) gift taxes

68. Inheritance taxes are levied by

(A) states on the beneficiaries of the estate
(B) the federal government on the beneficiaries of the estate
(C) states on the estate itself
(D) the federal government on the estate itself

69. Estate taxes are levied by

(A) the federal government on the estate itself
(B) states on the estate itself
(C) the federal government on the beneficiaries of the estate
(D) states on the beneficiaries of the estate

70. The dollar level at which estate taxes start is

(A) $100,000
(B) $30,000
(C) $60,000
(D) $150,000

71. Each individual has one lifetime exemption under gift taxes provisions of

(A) $60,000
(B) $3,000
(C) $10,000
(D) $30,000

72. The annual exemption permitted under the gift tax provision is

(A) $3,000 per donor per year
(B) $3,000 per person per year
(C) $5,000 per donor per year
(D) $5,000 per person per year

73. The lifetime exemption from the gift tax provisions can be given in

(A) several amounts in a year
(B) one amount in a year
(C) several amounts over a number of years
(D) any of the above manners

74. Under current IRS provisions, the maximum taxation of a corporation is

(A) nothing — only individuals pay taxes
(B) higher than the maximum taxation of an individual
(C) the same as the maximum taxation of an individual
(D) lower than the maximum taxation of an individual

75. Economists group indices as to whether they lead the economy, are coincident with the economy, or lag the economy. One of the foremost leading economic indicators is

(A) capital expenditures by industries
(B) the stock market
(C) consumer debt
(D) labor costs

CORRECT ANSWERS TO ELEMENTS OF FINANCE

Number in parenthesis, after answer, identifies number of reference source where information relating to the question and correct answer may be found.

1. C (7)	16. D (7)	31. A (3)	46. C (3)	61. A (9)
2. A (7)	17. C (3)	32. C (3)	47. A (3)	62. A (9)
3. A (7)	18. A (3)	33. D (3)	48. A (3)	63. C (9)
4. B (7)	19. B (3)	34. A (3)	49. A (3)	64. A (9)
5. A (7)	20. B (3)	35. B (3)	50. A (3)	65. D (9)
6. A (7)	21. A (7)	36. C (3)	51. D (7)	66. D (9)
7. A (3)	22. A (3)	37. D (3)	52. A (4)	67. A (8)
8. A (3)	23. D (3)	38. A (3)	53. B (4)	68. A (8)
9. D (7)	24. C (3)	39. A (3)	54. A (4)	69. A (8)
10. A (3)	25. A (3)	40. B (3)	55. B (4)	70. C (8)
11. A (3)	26. A (3)	41. A (3)	56. D (4)	71. D (8)
12. A (3)	27. D (3)	42. C (3)	57. A (4)	72. A (8)
13. C (3)	28. B (3)	43. A (3)	58. C (4)	73. D (8)
14. A (7)	29. A (3)	44. D (3)	59. A (4)	74. D (8)
15. A (3)	30. A (3)	45. A (3)	60. C (4)	75. B (7)

LIST OF REFERENCES

1. *New York Stock Exchange Constitution & Rules,* New York Stock Exchange, New York, N. Y.
2. *NASD Manual,* National Association of Securities Dealers, Washington, D. C.
3. *NASD Training Guide,* National Association of Securities Dealers, Washington, D. C.
4. *Fundamentals of the Money Market,* New York Stock Exchange, New York, N. Y.
5. *How to Invest on a Budget — MIP (Monthly Investment Plan),* New York Stock Exchange, New York, N. Y.
6. *The Interpretation of Financial Statements,* Graham & McGolrick — Harper & Row, Publishers, New York, N. Y.
7. *The Stock Market,* Leffler, Farwell — Ronald Press Company, New York, N. Y.
8. *Securities* — Volume 2, Second Edition; *Financial Planning and Mutual Funds,* Kalb, Voorhis & Co., New York, N. Y.
9. *Your Federal Income Tax,* Internal Revenue Service — Production Company, Scarborough, New York.
10. *Manual for Registered Representatives,* Association of Stock Exchange Firms (ASEF), New York, N. Y.
11. *American Stock Exchange Constitution,* American Stock Exchange, New York, N. Y.

ARCO PRACTICE ANSWER SHEET

2. Analysis of Securities

USE THE SPECIAL PENCIL. MAKE GLOSSY BLACK MARKS.

1	A	B	C	D	26	A	B	C	D	51	A	B	C	D
2	A	B	C	D	27	A	B	C	D	52	A	B	C	D
3	A	B	C	D	28	A	B	C	D	53	A	B	C	D
4	A	B	C	D	29	A	B	C	D	54	A	B	C	D
5	A	B	C	D	30	A	B	C	D	55	A	B	C	D
6	A	B	C	D	31	A	B	C	D	56	A	B	C	D
7	A	B	C	D	32	A	B	C	D	57	A	B	C	D
8	A	B	C	D	33	A	B	C	D	58	A	B	C	D
9	A	B	C	D	34	A	B	C	D	59	A	B	C	D
10	A	B	C	D	35	A	B	C	D	60	A	B	C	D
11	A	B	C	D	36	A	B	C	D	61	A	B	C	D
12	A	B	C	D	37	A	B	C	D	62	A	B	C	D
13	A	B	C	D	38	A	B	C	D	63	A	B	C	D
14	A	B	C	D	39	A	B	C	D	64	A	B	C	D
15	A	B	C	D	40	A	B	C	D	65	A	B	C	D
16	A	B	C	D	41	A	B	C	D	66	A	B	C	D
17	A	B	C	D	42	A	B	C	D	67	A	B	C	D
18	A	B	C	D	43	A	B	C	D	68	A	B	C	D
19	A	B	C	D	44	A	B	C	D	69	A	B	C	D
20	A	B	C	D	45	A	B	C	D	70	A	B	C	D
21	A	B	C	D	46	A	B	C	D	71	A	B	C	D
22	A	B	C	D	47	A	B	C	D	72	A	B	C	D
23	A	B	C	D	48	A	B	C	D	73	A	B	C	D
24	A	B	C	D	49	A	B	C	D	74	A	B	C	D
25	A	B	C	D	50	A	B	C	D	75	A	B	C	D

2. Analysis of Securities

1. The operating efficiency of a business can be determined by its

   (A) margin of profits
   (B) assets less its liabilities
   (C) sales less its liabilities
   (D) average inventory

2. The margin of profit is computed by dividing

   (A) operating income into net sales
   (B) net sales into operating income
   (C) operating income into gross sales
   (D) gross sales by earnings per share

3. Tests of earning power of a corporation include

   (A) fixed charge coverage of bonds
   (B) the current ratio
   (C) the acid test
   (D) inventory turnover

4. Working capital equals

   (A) surplus minus paid-in-capital
   (B) gross sales minus operating expenses
   (C) assets minus liabilities
   (D) current assets minus current liabilities

5. When working capital is expressed as a ratio, it is called

   (A) net quick ratio
   (B) the acid test
   (C) the current ratio
   (D) the dividend payout ratio

6. For an industrial type corporation, the minimum satisfactory current ratio is considered to be

   (A) 5 to 1
   (B) 1 to 1
   (C) 4 to 1
   (D) 2 to 1

7. The net quick ratio is defined as

   (A) current assets less inventories divided by current liabilities
   (B) fixed assets less current assets divided by total liabilities
   (C) working capital plus earned surplus
   (D) operating income divided by depreciation

8. Capitalization of a corporation is the

   (A) total dollar amount of all securities issued by the company
   (B) equity securities issued by the company, expressed in a ratio
   (C) debt securities issued by the company
   (D) number of shares of stocks and bonds issued by the corporation

9. The division of the capitalization of a company among bonds, preferred stocks, and common stock is the corporation's

   (A) net worth

(B) working capital
(C) capital structure
(D) surplus

10. A highly leveraged corporation would be one with a

(A) large amount of debt securities
(B) small amount of debt securities
(C) small amount of preferred stock
(D) large amount of preferred stock

11. Cash flow can be defined as

(A) net income plus depreciation
(B) net income minus depreciation
(C) current assets minus fixed assets
(D) current assets minus current liabilities

12. Inventory turnover is found by dividing inventory into

(A) expenses
(B) cost of goods sold
(C) operating income
(D) sales

13. The inventory turnover ratio indicates the

(A) liquidity of the inventory
(B) cost of the inventory
(C) profitability of the inventory
(D) carrying costs of the inventory

14. What is the price earnings ratio of a stock offered to the public at $20 per share, having current book value of $30 per share, and current market value of $45 per share. Its earnings are $3 per share and it paid dividends of $1 per share with a cash flow of $5 per share.

(A) 20:1
(B) 10:1
(C) 9:1
(D) 15:1

15. A corporation has 1,000,000 shares of common stock outstanding. Earnings after taxes were $1,000,000. The market price of the common stock is currently $20. The price earnings ratio of the common stock is

(A) 15 to 1
(B) 20 to 1
(C) 1.5 to 1
(D) 5 to 1

16. The amount of money actually paid out as dividends on common stock when expressed as a ratio is called the

(A) dividend pay out ratio
(B) dividend rate of return ratio
(C) earnings per share
(D) working capital

17. What is the annual dividend of a stock with a current market price of 36, a 9:1 PE ratio, and a dividend pay out ratio of 25%.

(A) $9
(B) $2
(C) $4
(D) $1

18. The yield in the above example would be

(A) 2%
(B) 5.56%
(C) 4%
(D) 2.78%

19. What is the yield on a stock currently selling at 50 which earned $4 per share and pays a quarterly dividend of $.50?

(A) 8%
(B) 4%
(C) 10%
(D) 12.5%

20. The value of the assets available for a stock issue after deducting all liabilities is called

(A) book value
(B) liquidating value
(C) market price
(D) stated value

21. All of the following could be typical of a special situation *except*:

(A) high earnings
(B) turnaround under new management

(C) large tax losses
(D) new technological breakthrough or new product

22. Which of the following would most likely have a lengthy record of payments of dividends?

(A) blue chip stocks
(B) growth stocks
(C) special situations
(D) debentures

23. An example of a defensive stock issue would be

(A) a mutual fund
(B) a new issue
(C) an issue having large contracts with the U. S. government
(D) a utility company

24. The general practice in computing book value is to

(A) include intangibles
(B) exclude intangibles
(C) express it as a ratio
(D) express it as a percentage

25. When a stock splits 2 for 1, the shareholders' interest

(A) has decreased 50%
(B) has increased 100%
(C) remains the same
(D) has increased 50%

26. A stock is selling at 50 and is offered to shareholders at 40 with four rights necessary to subscribe to one new share. The theoretical value of one right *before* the stock goes ex-rights is

(A) $10.00
(B) $2.50
(C) $2.00
(D) $12.50

27. The current price of a stock ex-rights is 40. Shareholders can subscribe at 30 with 4 rights. The theoretical value of one right is:

(A) $1.00
(B) $2.00
(C) $2.50
(D) $3.33

28. In practice, the theoretical value of a stock right and the market value of the right

(A) do not have to be precisely the same
(B) must always be exactly the same
(C) are always different
(D) are not related at all

29. Which of the values of a stock right fluctuate?

(A) both the market and theoretical value
(B) the market value
(C) the theoretical value
(D) neither the market nor the theoretical value

30. In evaluating certain securities, one of the things examined is fixed charge coverage. This is calculated by

(A) dividing income (before interest) by fixed charges
(B) subtracting income (before interest) from fixed charges
(C) subtracting current assets from current liabilities
(D) dividing net sales by income (before interest)

31. Fixed charge coverage is of primary interest to

(A) the bondholders of that issue
(B) common stockholders
(C) the specialist in that stock
(D) the NYSE Stock List Department

32. An acceptable standard of fixed charge coverage for industrial companies is

(A) 2 times earnings
(B) 7 times earnings
(C) 4 times earnings
(D) 11 times earnings

33. Preferred dividend coverage is computed by dividing income (before interest) by the sum of interest

    (A) plus 2 times the preferred dividend
    (B) plus the preferred dividends
    (C) minus the preferred dividends
    (D) minus 2 times the preferred dividends

34. Preferred dividends are paid

    (A) before common stock but after bondholders
    (B) before common stock and bondholders
    (C) after common stock and bondholders
    (D) after common stock but before bondholders

35. Interest on debt securities is deducted from

    (A) sales after taxes
    (B) income after taxes
    (C) income before taxes
    (D) sales before taxes

36. Dividends on preferred stock are paid from

    (A) net income before taxes
    (B) net income after taxes
    (C) working capital before taxes
    (D) retained earnings before taxes

37. A commonly accepted measure of the safety of a debt issue is its

    (A) rating by a service such as Standard & Poor's
    (B) current market price
    (C) current yield
    (D) maturity date

38. Corporate bonds

    (A) have a definite maturity date
    (B) pay dividends
    (C) represent ownership
    (D) are as safe as government securities

39. If a corporation calls an issue of bonds, the shareholder

    (A) may gain or lose depending on the price he paid for the issue and the call price
    (B) always gains as he receives face value
    (C) always loses if he bought at par
    (D) receives the face value of the certificate plus interest to maturity date

40. Convertible issues are possible in issues of

    (A) bonds or preferred stock
    (B) bonds or common stock
    (C) preferred or common stock
    (D) common stock only

41. The convertible features of issues can be exercised at the option of the

    (A) member firm
    (B) issuer
    (C) distributor
    (D) holder

42. That price where the common stock price is the same as the quotation for a convertible issue is called

    (A) parity
    (B) precedence
    (C) par
    (D) preference

43. If a $1,000 bond is convertible into 25 shares of common stock, the conversion price of the stock is

    (A) $5 a share
    (B) $50 a share
    (C) $25 a share
    (D) $40 a share

44. If a $100 par preferred stock is convertible into 4 shares of common stock and sells at 80, the conversion parity for the common would be

    (A) 25
    (B) 20
    (C) 10
    (D) 8

45. A $1,000 bond purchased at 105 would have been purchased at

    (A) a premium

(B) a discount
(C) par
(D) parity

46. The yield which takes into account the eventual gain or loss due to maturity of a debt issue is called

(A) yield to maturity
(B) current yield
(C) stated yield
(D) straight yield

47. The current yield of a 5% face bond bought at 120 is

(A) 4%
(B) 5%
(C) 6%
(D) unable to determine from this information

48. Dividing the annual interest by the current market price of a bond gives you

(A) face yield
(B) yield to maturity
(C) stated yield
(D) current yield

49. Bonds may not be offered for sale to the public unless the

(A) bonds are issued under a trust indenture
(B) client receives a prospectus
(C) member firm acts as principal
(D) member firm acts as broker

50. The document that describes in detail the rights and duties of an issuing corporation of debt securities is called

(A) prospectus
(B) confirmation
(C) deed of trust
(D) offering circular

51. The trustee under the Trustee Indenture Act of 1939 is usually

(A) the issuing company
(B) a bank
(C) the member firm doing the underwriting
(D) a committee of bondholders of that issue

52. An industry that is influenced by the ups and downs of the economy would be called

(A) a defensive industry
(B) a growth industry
(C) a cyclical industry
(D) an obsolete industry

53. Reasons that a whole industry could decline are any of the following *except*:

(A) number of shares traded
(B) competition
(C) labor costs or problems
(D) automation

54. Price earnings ratios have validity for comparing

(A) companies within one industry
(B) companies within different industries
(C) one industry group with another
(D) any stock

55. Technical analysis of the market would be most interested in the

(A) earnings per share of a stock
(B) price movement of stock
(C) marketing outlet for the company's products
(D) current yield of a company's bonds

56. Factors in technical analysis include all of the following *except*:

(A) book value of a particular stock
(B) breadth of the market
(C) volume of a particular stock
(D) the number of new highs and new lows

57. Breadth of market is defined as the

(A) number of shares traded
(B) number of issues traded
(C) difference between the number of issues which advanced subtracted from the number which declined
(D) number of new highs subtracted from the number of new lows

58. The fundamental approach to stock analysis would be least concerned with which of the following?

    (A) the maturity dates of a company's bonds
    (B) a company's management
    (C) an industry's future outlook
    (D) the profit centers of a company

59. Measures of the market that are based on a fairly large number of stocks and involve sophisticated statistical assistance are called

    (A) quotations
    (B) averages
    (C) theories
    (D) indexes

60. The Dow Jones Industrial Average is based on

    (A) all stocks listed on the NYSE
    (B) 50 stocks listed on NYSE
    (C) 15 stocks listed on NYSE
    (D) 30 stocks listed on NYSE

61. The NYSE Index is based on

    (A) all common and preferred stock listed on NYSE
    (B) all common stocks listed on NYSE
    (C) all issues listed on NYSE
    (D) representative issues listed on NYSE

62. Which of the following is indicative of a bull market?

    (A) rising volume in an up market
    (B) falling volume in an up market
    (C) rising volume in a down market
    (D) falling volume in a down market

63. The short interest is published by the NYSE and AMEX

    (A) weekly
    (B) daily
    (C) monthly
    (D) quarterly

64. According to the short selling theory, an increase in the short position of a stock

    (A) is a bearish sign
    (B) is a bullish sign
    (C) means the stock will go up by 10% of the amount of the increase
    (D) means that the stock will go down by 10% of the amount of the increase

65. The theory that says one portion of investors is always wrong by buying at the highs and selling at the lows is the

    (A) odd lot theory
    (B) Dow theory
    (C) short sell theory
    (D) custodian theory

66. The Dow theory is based on interpretations of the action of the Dow Jones

    (A) industrial and rail averages
    (B) industrial, rail and public utility averages
    (C) industrial average only
    (D) rail average only

67. Of the movements assumed under the Dow theory, the most important is

    (A) hourly fluctuations
    (B) the secondary movement
    (C) the daily fluctuations
    (D) the primary movement

68. If the Dow Jones industrial average were at 942, at which of the following could there be a resistance zone?

    (A) 930
    (B) 940
    (C) 950
    (D) 920

69. Support levels for ICI might be found at what price if ICI has a current market price of 35½?

    (A) 37⅞
    (B) 35⅝
    (C) 36⅜
    (D) 33¼

70. Overall, in analysis of debt instruments the highest degree of safety would be afforded by obligations of

    (A) the U. S. government

(B) municipalities
(C) revenue bonds
(D) corporate bonds

71. The element of the securities business that is involved in tailoring investment programs to specific individuals is called

(A) market analysis
(B) security analysis
(C) investment analysis
(D) portfolio analysis

72. Generally, the main investment objective of a young married couple would probably be a portfolio orientated toward

(A) growth
(B) income
(C) preservation of capital
(D) high speculation and risk

73. Investments in the stock market should be undertaken only

(A) with excess funds which could be lost
(B) before adequate life insurance is obtained
(C) before an emergency fund has been established
(D) based on tips or rumors heard in the office

74. The procedure of investing a fixed amount of money in a particular security at specific times is called

(A) dollar cost averaging
(B) averaging the dollar
(C) constant dollar plan
(D) scale trading

75. The formula investing plan where a set number of dollars are invested in stock and a set number of dollars invested in preferred stock or bonds is called

(A) scale trading
(B) dollar averaging
(C) dollar cost averaging
(D) a constant dollar plan

CORRECT ANSWERS TO ANALYSIS OF SECURITIES

Number in parenthesis, after answer, identifies number of reference source where information relating to the question and correct answer may be found.

1. A (3)	16. A (3)	31. A (3)	46. A (6)	61. B (3)
2. B (3)	17. D (3)	32. B (3)	47. A (6)	62. A (7)
3. A (3)	18. D (3)	33. A (3)	48. D (3)	63. C (7)
4. D (3)	19. B (3)	34. A (7)	49. A (3)	64. B (3)
5. C (3)	20. A (3)	35. C (3)	50. C (3)	65. A (7)
6. D (3)	21. A (3)	36. B (7)	51. B (3)	66. A (7)
7. A (3)	22. A (3)	37. A (3)	52. C (7)	67. D (7)
8. A (3)	23. D (3)	38. A (7)	53. A (7)	68. C (7)
9. C (3)	24. B (3)	39. A (7)	54. A (3)	69. D (7)
10. A (7)	25. C (3)	40. A (6)	55. B (7)	70. A (3)
11. A (3)	26. C (7)	41. D (7)	56. A (7)	71. D (3)
12. D (3)	27. C (7)	42. A (6)	57. B (7)	72. A (3)
13. A (3)	28. A (7)	43. D (6)	58. A (7)	73. A (7)
14. B (3)	29. A (7)	44. B (7)	59. D (7)	74. A (7)
15. B (3)	30. A (3)	45. A (7)	60. D (7)	75. D (7)

LIST OF REFERENCES

1. *New York Stock Exchange Constitution & Rules,* New York Stock Exchange, New York, N. Y.
2. *NASD Manual,* National Association of Securities Dealers, Washington, D. C.
3. *NASD Training Guide,* National Association of Securities Dealers, Washington, D. C.
4. *Fundamentals of the Money Market,* New York Stock Exchange, New York, N. Y.
5. *How to Invest on a Budget — MIP (Monthly Investment Plan),* New York Stock Exchange, New York, N. Y.
6. *The Interpretation of Financial Statements,* Graham & McGolrick — Harper & Row, Publishers, New York, N. Y.
7. *The Stock Market,* Leffler, Farwell — Ronald Press Company, New York, N. Y.
8. *Securities* — Volume 2, Second Edition; *Financial Planning and Mutual Funds,* Kalb, Voorhis & Co., New York, N. Y.
9. *Your Federal Income Tax,* Internal Revenue Service — Production Company, Scarborough, New York.
10. *Manual for Registered Representatives,* Association of Stock Exchange Firms (ASEF), New York, N. Y.
11. *American Stock Exchange Constitution,* American Stock Exchange, New York, N. Y.

ARCO PRACTICE ANSWER SHEET

3. Investment Companies

USE THE SPECIAL PENCIL. MAKE GLOSSY BLACK MARKS.

1 A B C D
2 A B C D
3 A B C D
4 A B C D
5 A B C D
6 A B C D
7 A B C D
8 A B C D
9 A B C D
10 A B C D
11 A B C D
12 A B C D
13 A B C D
14 A B C D
15 A B C D
16 A B C D
17 A B C D
18 A B C D
19 A B C D
20 A B C D
21 A B C D
22 A B C D
23 A B C D
24 A B C D
25 A B C D
26 A B C D
27 A B C D
28 A B C D
29 A B C D
30 A B C D
31 A B C D
32 A B C D
33 A B C D
34 A B C D
35 A B C D
36 A B C D
37 A B C D
38 A B C D
39 A B C D
40 A B C D
41 A B C D
42 A B C D
43 A B C D
44 A B C D
45 A B C D
46 A B C D
47 A B C D
48 A B C D
49 A B C D
50 A B C D
51 A B C D
52 A B C D
53 A B C D
54 A B C D
55 A B C D
56 A B C D
57 A B C D
58 A B C D
59 A B C D
60 A B C D
61 A B C D
62 A B C D
63 A B C D
64 A B C D
65 A B C D
66 A B C D
67 A B C D
68 A B C D
69 A B C D
70 A B C D
71 A B C D
72 A B C D
73 A B C D
74 A B C D
75 A B C D

3. Investment Companies

1. The pooling of funds by investors to obtain diversification and supervision of investments is done through buying

   (A) one MIP plan
   (B) an individual stock
   (C) an individual bond
   (D) a mutual fund

2. The type of investment company that issues a specific number of shares and no more is called

   (A) an open end fund
   (B) a closed end fund
   (C) a mutual fund
   (D) a diversified common stock fund

3. The type of investment company which might be listed on an organized exchange is

   (A) a mutual fund
   (B) an open end fund
   (C) a closed end fund
   (D) a diversified common stock fund

4. Characteristics of a mutual fund include all of the following *except*:

   (A) addition of a commission charge to the public offering price
   (B) ability to redeem securities at any time
   (C) continued offering of shares
   (D) sale of shares by prospectus

5. Which of the following is a closed end type of investment company?

   (A) income fund
   (B) balanced fund
   (C) diversified common stock fund
   (D) dual purpose fund

6. The mutual fund which always has some of its assets in debt securities as well as equities is the

   (A) dual purpose fund
   (B) balanced fund
   (C) income fund
   (D) specialized fund

7. A fund that states it intends to invest in a single industry would be a

   (A) specialized fund
   (B) balanced fund
   (C) diversified common stock fund
   (D) income fund

8. A type of fund which has a "leverage" factor in it is the

   (A) dual purpose fund
   (B) balanced fund
   (C) specialized fund
   (D) diversified common stock fund

9. The type of investment companies that could issue debt securities is the

(A) specialized fund
(B) open end fund
(C) balanced fund
(D) closed end fund

10. Management fees of a mutual fund are paid by the

(A) fund to the management company
(B) management company to the fund
(C) purchaser of the fund to the fund
(D) wholesaler of the fund to the fund

11. Typically the management fee is about

(A) ½ of 1% of the average daily net assets of the fund for a year
(B) 1% of the average daily net assets of the fund for a year
(C) 1½% of the average daily net assets of the fund for a year
(D) 5% of the average daily net assets of the fund for a year

12. Operating expenses plus management fees would typically amount to what percent of the fund's assets?

(A) 5%
(B) ½ of 1%
(C) 2%
(D) 1%

13. Normally the custodian function for a mutual fund is performed by

(A) the fund itself
(B) a national bank
(C) the fund's management company
(D) the fund's distributor

14. The price at which a fund having a sales charge can be redeemed is the

(A) asked price
(B) public offering price
(C) net asset value
(D) book value

15. The sales charge for a mutual fund is stated as a percentage of the

(A) book value
(B) net asset value
(C) bid price
(D) public offering price

16. Which of the following is not a part of net investment income for a mutual fund?

(A) interest from debt securities in the portfolio
(B) dividends from common stocks in the portfolio
(C) dividends from preferred stocks in the portfolio
(D) short term capital gain on sale of securities in the portfolio

17. Typically capital gain distributions of a mutual fund are

(A) considered a return of capital
(B) treated as short term gains for tax purposes
(C) taken out in cash
(D) reinvested at public offering price

18. To be a "regulated investment company" a mutual fund must distribute at least

(A) 90% of its net investment income
(B) 60% of its net investment income
(C) 50% of its net investment income
(D) 25% of its net investment income

19. The agency which sets up the requirements for a regulated investment company is the

(A) NYSE
(B) SEC
(C) Internal Revenue Service
(D) NASD

20. In addition to distributing at least a specific percentage of its net investment income each year, a regulated investment company must obtain what percent of its gross income during the year from interest, dividends, and gains from securities?

(A) 60%
(B) 90%

(C) 50%
(D) 25%

21. Classified as investment companies under the 1940 Act are:

(A) face amount certificate companies
(B) groups who band together to buy securities as a unit
(C) insurance companies
(D) mutual funds having 33% of their assets in securities

22. The type of investment company which has a guarantee of both interest and principal is

(A) a face-amount certificate company
(B) a mutual fund
(C) a unit investment trust
(D) non-existant, as all investment company issues have risk

23. A diversified company under the 1940 Act must have (_____) % of its assets invested in such a way that not more than (_____) % of its total assets are invested in one company, nor more than (_____) % of the outstanding voting securities of any one issue are owned by the company

(A) 75% — 5% — 10%
(B) 75% — 10% — 5%
(C) 90% — 10% — 5%
(D) 90% — 5% — 10%

24. Registered Investment Companies must file under the Federal Acts of

(A) 1940 and 1933
(B) 1940 only
(C) 1933 only
(D) 1940 and 1934

25. The Board of Directors of a registered investment company must consist of at least what percent of members from beyond the company or its affiliates?

(A) 60%
(B) 50%
(C) 40%
(D) 90%

26. To make a public offering, a registered investment company must have a net worth of at least

(A) $500,000
(B) $1,000,000
(C) $100,000
(D) $5,000,000

27. A mutual fund can never

(A) issue senior securities
(B) make loans
(C) purchase real estate
(D) deal in commodities

28. All registered investment companies under the provision of the 1940 Act must file a certified audit report with the SEC

(A) quarterly
(B) semi-annually
(C) annually
(D) every 2 years

29. The document that must accompany every sale of a mutual fund is a

(A) due bill
(B) registration statement
(C) financial statement
(D) prospectus

30. The maximum sales load authorized for a periodic payment plan by the 1940 Act is

(A) 8.5%
(B) 8.75%
(C) 9%
(D) 8%

31. In redemption of a mutual fund, the amount obtained

(A) may be more or less than cost depending on the market price
(B) is always tax free
(C) is received from the management company
(D) is always subject to a commission charge

32. The net asset value of a mutual fund is now normally computed

(A) once a day
(B) twice a day
(C) once a week
(D) every month

33. Mutual funds may purchase securities on margin

(A) if their charter permits
(B) if their shareholders permit
(C) in no cases, as the NASD does not permit it
(D) in no cases, as the Investment Company Act of 1940 does not permit it

34. Net assets divided by the number of shares outstanding gives you

(A) the current market price of the fund
(B) the public offering price
(C) the asked price
(D) net asset value per share

35. In purchasing mutual funds, quantity discounts

(A) are acceptable business procedures
(B) are illegal under the NASD rules
(C) are illegal under the SEC rules
(D) are illegal under both SEC and NASD rules

36. A letter of intent is valid for a period of time not to exceed

(A) 6 months
(B) 12 months
(C) 10 months
(D) 13 months

37. Which of the following can not qualify for a reduced sales charge in purchasing mutual funds?

(A) an investment club
(B) an individual
(C) an individual, his wife and/or children under 21
(D) a fiduciary of a single trust estate

38. On redemption of an open end mutual fund, the fund must make payment within

(A) 4 days
(B) 5 days
(C) 7 days
(D) 10 days

39. Level sales charges are not associated with

(A) a contractual plan
(B) a voluntary accumulation plan
(C) reinvestment of capital gains
(D) an outright purchase

40. In a contractual plan, up to what percent of the first year's payment can be deducted for sales charges?

(A) 40%
(B) 50%
(C) 60%
(D) 9%

41. Another name for a contractual plan is

(A) withdrawal plan
(B) level pay plan
(C) volunteer plan
(D) front end load

42. Typically the basic rate that withdrawal plans return is

(A) 3%
(B) 10%
(C) 6%
(D) 12%

43. Breakpoint sales are the sale of mutual fund shares in an amount

(A) just below the dollar amount where the sales charge is reduced
(B) just above the dollar amount where the sales charge is reduced
(C) at the point where the sales charge is reduced
(D) below the public offering price of the fund

44. "These securities have not been approved or disapproved" is a phrase required to be shown in a prospectus by the

(A) NASD
(B) SEC
(C) NYSE
(D) management company

45. The Statement of Policy was issued by the

(A) Investment Company Act
(B) NASD
(C) NYSE
(D) SEC

46. According to the provisions of the SOP, "sales literature" includes

(A) any communication, even oral, that tends to induce the purchase of mutual funds
(B) communications between different mutual funds
(C) communications from selling group member to customers
(D) communications from a client to a mutual fund

47. Under the SOP provisions, the RR should explain all of the following *except*:

(A) the net asset value of the fund changes continually
(B) the past is no guide to the future
(C) income of the fund fluctuates each year
(D) our inflationary economic trend means mutual funds will perform better in the future

48. Under the SOP requirements, dividends from net investment income and distributions from other sources

(A) may not be combined into one account
(B) may be combined into one account
(C) must be combined into one account
(D) are not covered by the regulation

49. The right of the shareholder to change his holdings in one fund into another fund of the same management group is known as

(A) discounting the fund
(B) redemption of the fund
(C) a conversion privilege
(D) pre-emptive right

50. Which of the following *can* be said or used under the provision of the SOP?

(A) to use the phrase dollar cost averaging
(B) to state that mutual funds are direct sources of new capital to industry
(C) to state that management of a mutual fund is under the same restrictions as banks by government authorities
(D) to use any charts or tables which you might draw up to help in closing a mutual fund sale

51. If an investment company's offering price was lower than its net asset value per share, it must be a

(A) no load fund
(B) open end fund
(C) closed end fund
(D) balanced fund

52. From the following information, which is correct?

Fund	*Net asset value*	*Ask price*
A	12.12	12.12
B	10.00	10.75
C	10.75	10.00

(A) A is a no load fund; B-open end; C-closed end
(B) A is a no load fund; B-closed end; C-open end
(C) All three are open end funds
(D) A is closed end, B and C are open end

53. A discussion that mutual funds are strictly regulated should point out that

(A) this regulation guarantees a profit will be made
(B) SEC regulation protects against market risk
(C) there is no guarantee against risk due to this regulation
(D) this regulation insures the directors will make the right decision

54. The SOP permits the rate of return on a mutual fund to be presented
   (A) either on a historic or current basis
   (B) only on a historic basis
   (C) only on a current basis
   (D) as blend of either method

55. In presenting rates of return it is necessary to show the asset value per share at
   (A) the beginning and end of the period covered
   (B) the beginning of the period only
   (C) the end of the period only
   (D) either time, as you prefer

56. Which of the following is a permissible statement under the SOP provisions?
   (A) "XYZ is custodian for the fund"
   (B) "The cash and securities of the fund are held by the XYZ Bank and thus are safeguarded from decline"
   (C) "The cash and securities are protected by XYZ Bank as custodian"
   (D) "XYZ Bank supervises the investment of securities as custodian"

57. In connection with mutual funds, a sales agreement would be entered into between the
   (A) member firm and a prospective client
   (B) underwriter of a fund and a member firm
   (C) fund itself and a prospective client
   (D) fund itself and a member firm

58. The section of the Internal Revenue Code which permits special tax treatment of mutual funds is
   (A) Reg. U
   (B) Sub-chapter W
   (C) Reg. T
   (D) Sub-chapter M

59. The expense ratio of a mutual fund is the total expenses of the fund contrasted to the
   (A) public offering price of the fund
   (B) total income of the fund
   (C) total income and realized capital gains of the fund
   (D) total average net assets of the fund

60. One item that is not a part of the custodian function is to
   (A) maintain custody of the fund shares for individual owners
   (B) provide protection against depreciation of the fund's assets
   (C) provide the bookkeeping functions for the fund
   (D) act as dividend disbursing agent for the fund

61. The type of investment company which would not always have to be sold by prospectus is a
   (A) growth mutual fund
   (B) balanced fund
   (C) closed end fund
   (D) specialized mutual fund

62. The prospectus of a mutual fund shows the
   (A) dates of the annual shareholders meeting
   (B) portfolio positions of the fund for the past 10 years
   (C) assurance clause that risk will be minimum through investing in a mutual fund
   (D) fund's objectives

63. In the prospectus, securities positions of the fund are shown at
   (A) market price only
   (B) cost price only
   (C) market always, and sometimes cost too
   (D) cost or market, whichever is lower

64. It is the policy of most mutual funds to distribute
   (A) dividends quarterly and capital gains (if any) annually
   (B) dividends and capital gains (if any) quarterly
   (C) dividends and capital gains (if any) annually
   (D) dividends annually and capital gains (if any) quarterly

65. Which of the following will a prospectus of a mutual fund *not* show?
   (A) if automatic re-investment of dividends is possible

(B) whether plan completion insurance is available
(C) prices of securities positions changed during the period
(D) if a minimum initial investment is required in the fund

66. Plan completion insurance for a contractual plan will pay

(A) 150% of the unpaid balance to complete the contract upon death of the planholder
(B) the full face amount of the contract upon death of the planholder
(C) the difference between the then current market value of the plan and the face amount of the plan
(D) the unpaid balance to complete the contract upon death of the planholder

67. The Keogh Act is a

(A) method of deferring taxes on current income for personnel of listed companies
(B) method of deferring taxes on current income for self-employed individuals
(C) method of profit sharing for RR's of member firms
(D) profit sharing plan for all self-employed individuals such as doctors, lawyers or accountants

68. Under the Keogh Act, qualified individuals can set aside annually up to

(A) $5000 or 5% of earned income, whichever is more
(B) $2500 or 5% of earned income, whichever is more
(C) $2500 or 10% of earned income, whichever is less
(D) $5000 or 10% of earned income, whichever is less

69. Typically a regulated investment company pays taxes on

(A) its net income
(B) its total investment income
(C) its undistributed net income
(D) its distributed net income

70. In a withdrawal plan, a client should be told

(A) that there is an inherent risk of his capital being depleted
(B) that the fund guarantees the payment of 6% per year
(C) that besides a 6% rate per year, his capital is sure to grow
(D) the plan is just the same as an annuity

71. After the initial distribution, closed end funds are bought from

(A) the investment company
(B) the underwriters
(C) the management company
(D) shareholders who wish to sell

72. The type of investment company which could sell at a premium or discount is a(n)

(A) mutual fund
(B) open end fund
(C) closed end fund
(D) any of the above

73. Reasons for investing in a mutual fund include all of the following *except*:

(A) lack of any risk
(B) the professional management of the fund
(C) diversification of portfolio
(D) ability to liquidate shares easily

74. Typically a no load fund is purchased

(A) directly from the underwriter
(B) directly from the shareholder who desires to sell
(C) through an NYSE member firm who buys it from the management company
(D) through an NYSE member firm who buys it from the investment company

75. When using charts or tables, the SOP requires that they cover the life of the fund or the immediate preceding

(A) 5 years, whichever is smaller
(B) 5 years, whichever is greater
(C) 10 years, whichever is smaller
(D) 10 years, whichever is greater

CORRECT ANSWERS TO INVESTMENT COMPANIES

Number in parenthesis, after answer, identifies number of reference source where information relating to the question and correct answer may be found.

1. D (8)	16. D (3)	31. A (8)	46. A (8)	61. C (3)
2. B (8)	17. A (3)	32. A (8)	47. D (8)	62. D (8)
3. C (8)	18. A (8)	33. D (3)	48. A (3)	63. C (8)
4. A (8)	19. C (8)	34. D (3)	49. C (3)	64. A (8)
5. D (3)	20. B (8)	35. A (8)	50. A (8)	65. C (8)
6. B (3)	21. A (3)	36. D (3)	51. C (3)	66. D (8)
7. A (3)	22. A (3)	37. A (3)	52. A (3)	67. B (8)
8. A (3)	23. A (3)	38. C (3)	53. C (8)	68. C (8)
9. D (8)	24. A (8)	39. A (8)	54. A (8)	69. C (8)
10. A (8)	25. C (8)	40. B (8)	55. A (8)	70. A (8)
11. A (3)	26. C (8)	41. D (3)	56. A (3)	71. D (8)
12. D (3)	27. A (8)	42. C (8)	57. B (8)	72. C (8)
13. B (3)	28. C (8)	43. A (3)	58. D (8)	73. A (8)
14. C (3)	29. D (8)	44. B (8)	59. D (8)	74. A (8)
15. B (3)	30. C (8)	45. D (8)	60. B (8)	75. D (8)

LIST OF REFERENCES

1. *New York Stock Exchange Constitution & Rules,* New York Stock Exchange, New York, N. Y.
2. *NASD Manual,* National Association of Securities Dealers, Washington, D. C.
3. *NASD Training Guide,* National Association of Securities Dealers, Washington, D. C.
4. *Fundamentals of the Money Market,* New York Stock Exchange, New York, N. Y.
5. *How to Invest on a Budget — MIP (Monthly Investment Plan),* New York Stock Exchange, New York, N. Y.
6. *The Interpretation of Financial Statements,* Graham & McGolrick — Harper & Row, Publishers, New York, N. Y.
7. *The Stock Market,* Leffler, Farwell — Ronald Press Company, New York, N. Y.
8. *Securities* — Volume 2, Second Edition; *Financial Planning and Mutual Funds,* Kalb, Voorhis & Co., New York, N. Y.
9. *Your Federal Income Tax,* Internal Revenue Service — Production Company, Scarborough, New York.
10. *Manual for Registered Representatives,* Association of Stock Exchange Firms (ASEF), New York, N. Y.
11. *American Stock Exchange Constitution,* American Stock Exchange, New York, N. Y.

ARCO PRACTICE ANSWER SHEET

4. Securities Business Procedures

USE THE SPECIAL PENCIL. MAKE GLOSSY BLACK MARKS.

1 A B C D
2 A B C D
3 A B C D
4 A B C D
5 A B C D
6 A B C D
7 A B C D
8 A B C D
9 A B C D
10 A B C D
11 A B C D
12 A B C D
13 A B C D
14 A B C D
15 A B C D
16 A B C D
17 A B C D
18 A B C D
19 A B C D
20 A B C D
21 A B C D
22 A B C D
23 A B C D
24 A B C D
25 A B C D
26 A B C D
27 A B C D
28 A B C D
29 A B C D
30 A B C D
31 A B C D
32 A B C D
33 A B C D
34 A B C D
35 A B C D
36 A B C D
37 A B C D
38 A B C D
39 A B C D
40 A B C D
41 A B C D
42 A B C D
43 A B C D
44 A B C D
45 A B C D
46 A B C D
47 A B C D
48 A B C D
49 A B C D
50 A B C D
51 A B C D
52 A B C D
53 A B C D
54 A B C D
55 A B C D
56 A B C D
57 A B C D
58 A B C D
59 A B C D
60 A B C D
61 A B C D
62 A B C D
63 A B C D
64 A B C D
65 A B C D
66 A B C D
67 A B C D
68 A B C D
69 A B C D
70 A B C D
71 A B C D
72 A B C D
73 A B C D
74 A B C D
75 A B C D

4. Securities Business Procedures

1. A firm acting as a broker is in the legal capacity of a(n)

   (A) representative
   (B) principal
   (C) dealer
   (D) agent

2. The corporate affiliates of an NYSE member firm may

   (A) conduct an investment advisor business
   (B) act as broker
   (C) carry customers' accounts
   (D). hold securities for clients

3. One of the things which a guaranteed corporate subsidiary of an NYSE member firm may *not* do is

   (A) to hold customers' funds
   (B) conduct an underwriting business
   (C) operate a foreign branch
   (D) conduct principal transactions

4. The Net Capital Rule of the SEC requires that a securities firm must not permit its

   (A) "net capital" to exceed 2000% of its liabilities
   (B) "net capital" to exceed 2000% of its "aggregate indebtedness"
   (C) liabilities to exceed 2000% of its "net capital"
   (D) "aggregate indebtedness" to exceed 2000% of its "net capital"

5. In computing the net capital of a firm, furniture and fixtures are

   (A) considered a part of "net capital"
   (B) considered a part of current assets
   (C) considered a part of "aggregated indebtedness"
   (D) not considered a part of current assets

6. The minimum capital of securities firms under SEC Rule 15C 3-1 is

   (A) $5,000
   (B) $2,500
   (C) $25,000
   (D) $50,000

7. In computing net capital, securities held in the firm's account are

   (A) included at something less than current market price, i.e. with a hair cut
   (B) not computed at all
   (C) computed at cost
   (D) computed at current market level

8. In opening an account, the one document that is always necessary is a

   (A) signature card
   (B) cash account agreement
   (C) margin agreement
   (D) new account form

9. A husband and wife wish to open a securities account. Which of the following is *not* permitted?

   (A) open an account for each of them; and,

as they are married, each can enter orders for the other as a normal course of business
(B) open an account in either name with power of attorney for one to act for the other
(C) open a joint account
(D) each open a separate account and operate it separately

10. Accounts in the name of a minor
(A) are common and acceptable
(B) may be opened if guaranteed by an adult
(C) should not be opened
(D) are a fine way to develop clientele

11. Which of the following is an acceptable account for a minor?
(A) John Ringer as custodian for Jay Ringer, a minor
(B) John and Nancy Ringer as custodian for Jay Ringer, a minor
(C) John Ringer as custodian for Jay and Burton Ringer, minors
(D) None; accounts for minors can not be opened in any manner

12. Documents necessary to open an individual margin account are
(A) loan consent, signature card and new account form
(B) new account form, margin agreement and loan consent
(C) margin agreement and loan consent
(D) margin agreement, loan consent, new account form and power of attorney

13. The joint account where the remaining party retains his proportionate interest after death is called
(A) tenant in private
(B) joint account in common
(C) joint account with right of survivorship
(D) a tenant in common

14. The difference between a limited and full trading authorization is the ability in the full account to
(A) withdraw cash or securities
(B) buy *or* sell without contacting the client
(C) select the security for purchase without contacting the client
(D) enter limit orders rather than only market orders without contacting the client

15. To execute a discretionary order
(A) prior written authorization must be obtained from the client
(B) prior oral authorization must be obtained from the client
(C) a partner must approve every order in advance
(D) the RR must disclose if he is acting as principal in the trade

16. The concurrence of you as a client to settle any controversy arising out of the trades in an account through arbitration is part of the standard
(A) new account form
(B) loan consent
(C) customer's agreement
(D) signature card form

17. To permit the lending of securities, a customer must sign a
(A) loan consent
(B) margin agreement
(C) joint account agreement
(D) new account form

18. In opening a partnership account according to the ASEF Manual, it is
(A) not necessary to obtain a copy of the partnership agreement
(B) necessary to obtain a copy of the partnership agreement
(C) necessary to obtain a copy of the charter to show the state the firm is based in
(D) not necessary to obtain a new account form

19. Investment clubs are
(A) individuals who join together to pool their ideas and money

(B) the same as investment companies
(C) groups of registered personnel from different firms who invest collectively
(D) groups to which personnel from member firms who do investment banking belong

20. Every order at the time of entry must show all of the following *except* the

(A) date
(B) stock
(C) number of shares
(D) price

21. According to SEC rules, records of orders must be kept for a minimum of

(A) two years
(B) six years
(C) three years
(D) four years

22. Proxy material must be forwarded to the beneficial owner *except* when that owner

(A) lives outside the U.S.A.
(B) has asked that material not be sent
(C) has already sold the stock within the four days before record date
(D) says he has already voted

23. Stock transactions go ex-dividend on the

(A) 3rd business day before record date
(B) 4th business day before record date
(C) 3rd calendar day before record date
(D) 4th calendar day before record date

24. If a stock declared a dividend of .30, on the ex-date it would drop by

(A) 3/8
(B) .30
(C) 1/2
(D) 1/4

25. A stock closed at 40 1/8 after a previous sale at 40. It went ex-dividend by .25. The next day the lowest price at which a short sale could occur would be

(A) 39 7/8
(B) 40
(C) 40 1/8
(D) 40 1/4

26. Cash trades settle

(A) the 5th business day
(B) the next business day
(C) the next calendar day
(D) that same day

27. A cash trade

(A) may or may not be at the same price as the last regular way trade
(B) must be at the same price as the last regular way trade
(C) must be at least 1/2 point above the last regular way trade
(D) is never related to the regular way transaction

28. Seller option contracts call for delivery between the

(A) 6th business day and 60 calendar days from trade date
(B) 5th business day and 60 calendar days from trade date
(C) 5th business day and 60 business days from trade date
(D) 6th business day and 60 business days from trade date

29. The commissions charged by NYSE member firms are

(A) maximum rates
(B) minimum rates
(C) consistent at 1% of the dollar amount of the trade
(D) consistent at 1 1/2% of the dollar amount of the trade

30. State taxes on transactions are paid by the

(A) member firm
(B) buyer
(C) buyer and the seller
(D) seller

31. The NYSE commission rate on trades amounting to less than $100 is

(A) as mutually agreed

(B) $6 per trade
(C) 5% of the amount involved
(D) 7% of the amount involved

32. The NYSE *maximum* commission for a single round lot transaction is

(A) $150
(B) $100
(C) $75
(D) $200

33. Commission for odd lots of stock are computed the same as

(A) round lot trades
(B) round lot trades, less $5
(C) round lot trades, less 2%
(D) round lot trades, less $2

34. Typically the transfer of stock is accomplished by

(A) the NYSE
(B) the corporation itself
(C) the member firm
(D) a bank

35. If a party to a contract becomes partially unsecured by reason of a change in the market value of the stock, he would be

(A) marked to the market
(B) sold out
(C) bought in
(D) restricted in his account

36. When stock is registered in the name of a member firm rather than the beneficial owner, it is called

(A) fraud
(B) a bearer certificate
(C) a street name certificate
(D) a nominee name note

37. Stock held by a member firm in safekeeping is in

(A) the client's name
(B) the member firm's name
(C) street name
(D) a nominee's name

38. Confirmations of transactions are sent to clients by the

(A) purchase and sale department
(B) order department
(C) cashier
(D) account statement department

39. The processing of a stock certificate for transfer would be handled by personnel of the

(A) order room
(B) cage
(C) P & S area
(D) proxy department

40. The transmission of a listed trade to the floor of the Exchange is handled by the

(A) order department
(B) P & S department
(C) account department
(D) cage

41. Receipt of payment for a sale of securities would be accomplished by the

(A) order department
(B) account department
(C) P & S department
(D) cage

42. Which of the following can never be bought on margin?

(A) open end investment company shares
(B) closed end investment company shares
(C) municipal bonds
(D) listed stocks

43. Initial margin requirements originate under the provisions of the

(A) Securities Exchange Act of 1934
(B) Securities Act of 1933
(C) Rules of the NYSE
(D) SEC

44. To sell securities short, a client must have a

(A) non purpose loan account
(B) cash account
(C) special miscellaneous account
(D) margin account

45. The regulation which governs initial margin requirements is

(A) Regulation T
(B) Regulation A
(C) Regulation G
(D) Regulation U

46. Regulation T and Regulation U were issued by the

(A) ASEF
(B) SEC
(C) NYSE
(D) Federal Reserve Board

47. The initial maintenance margin requirement of the NYSE states that the minimum equity in a new margin account must be at least

(A) $2,500
(B) $1,000
(C) $2,000
(D) $5,000

48. Regulation T includes requirements with regard to

(A) discretionary accounts
(B) cash accounts only
(C) margin accounts only
(D) cash accounts and margin accounts

49. Regulation T states that transactions in a special cash account must be paid for promptly. Promptly is defined as payment being made within

(A) 10 business days
(B) 7 calendar days
(C) 10 calendar days
(D) 7 business days

50. Regulation T permits disregarding for extension purposes debit balances in a cash account which do not exceed

(A) $50
(B) $100
(C) $500
(D) $1,000

51. If exceptional circumstances have prevented a client from paying for securities within the prescribed time of Regulation T,

(A) the firm must sell out the account for the account and risk of the client
(B) the firm can ignore the non-payment and need take no action
(C) an extension of time can be requested
(D) the firm must sell out the account for the account and risk of the firm

52. The initial margin requirement on obligations of the U. S. government is

(A) 5% of the principal amount of the security
(B) 10% of the principal amount of the security
(C) 15% of the principal amount of the security, or 25% of the market value, whichever is lower
(D) 15% of the principal amount of the security, or 25% of the market value, whichever is higher

53. The initial margin requirement on exempt securities other than obligations of the U. S. government is

(A) 15% of the principal amount of the security, or 25% of the market value, whichever is higher
(B) 15% of the principal amount of the security, or 25% of the market value, whichever is lower
(C) 5% of the principal amount of the security
(D) 10% of the principal amount of the security

54. NYSE rules covering margin transactions are primarily concerned with

(A) special cash accounts
(B) initial requirements
(C) borrowing arrangements
(D) maintenance requirements

55. In a margin account, the amount borrowed from the member firm is called

(A) equity
(B) margin
(C) the debit balance
(D) the credit balance

56. The excess of current market value in a margin account over the amount owed is called the

(A) loan balance
(B) debit balance
(C) credit balance
(D) equity

57. The amount in an unrestricted margin account which a client can withdraw is called the

(A) loan value
(B) buying power
(C) debit balance
(D) excess

58. For Regulation T purposes, a listed stock is referred to as

(A) a registered security
(B) an unregistered security
(C) an exempt security
(D) a miscellaneous security

59. The dollar amount of registered securities which can be purchased by the excess in a margin account is called the

(A) equity
(B) margin
(C) buying power
(D) loan value

60. If a margin account has equity in excess of Regulation T requirements, such an account is termed

(A) an unrestricted account
(B) a restricted account
(C) a frozen account
(D) an exempt account

61. The purchase and sale of different stocks on the same day in a restricted account is called

(A) substitution
(B) freezing the account
(C) day trading
(D) fraud

62. If the margin requirement is at 80%, and you deposit $6,000 in market value of listed securities, your buying power for listed stocks would be

(A) $1,200
(B) $1,500
(C) $4,800
(D) $ 750

63. On a short sale of $6,000 dollar value of a listed stock, what is the amount of cash needed if margin requirements are at 80%?

(A) $7,500
(B) $1,500
(C) $1,200
(D) $4,800

64. If the margin requirement is 80% and you deposit $6,000, what is your buying power?

(A) $1,500
(B) $4,800
(C) $7,500
(D) $1,200

65. The pledging of customers' securities as collateral for loans with brokers or dealers is called

(A) rehypothecation
(B) hypothecation
(C) substitution
(D) fraud

66. Commingling of securities for loans of one customer with those of another client

(A) is illegal
(B) is permitted with prior written consent of the client
(C) is permitted for listed stocks only
(D) requires prior written consent of the NYSE

67. Commingling of securities in the account of one customer with those of general partners of a member firm

    (A) is illegal
    (B) is permitted with prior written consent of the client
    (C) is permitted for listed stocks only
    (D) requires prior written consent of the NYSE

68. The marking of fully paid for customers' securities in such a way that identifies the interest of each individual customer is called

    (A) hypothecation
    (B) marking to the market
    (C) segregation
    (D) rehypothecation

69. Blue sky laws is the term applied to

    (A) state securities regulations
    (B) NYSE rules and regulations
    (C) the ASEF rules and regulations
    (D) the SEC rules and regulations

70. Blue sky laws can be classified as being concerned with

    (A) activities of broker-dealers and/or anti-fraud provisions
    (B) regulation of the organized exchanges
    (C) upholding the NASD's rules
    (D) money and credit extensions

71. A candidate for registration approval by the NYSE and/or NASD

    (A) must still meet the registration requirements of the state(s) in which he expects to do business
    (B) must still meet the registration requirements of the states in which any branch offices are located
    (C) is automatically registered in those states shown on his NYSE and NASD applications
    (D) is automatically registered in the state in which his branch office is located

72. Institutional investors such as savings banks and trust funds generally must purchase securities from the states

    (A) blue list
    (B) legal list
    (C) pink sheets
    (D) uniform list

73. A fiduciary must make investments in accordance with the concept of the

    (A) blue sky rule
    (B) 5% rule
    (C) legal list rule
    (D) prudent man rule

74. Payments for securities sold through a broker-dealer are due to the client on the

    (A) 5th business day following sale
    (B) 5th calendar day following sale
    (C) day of sale
    (D) day after the sale

75. Prepayment by a member firm to a client

    (A) shall be reviewed promptly by a general partner/holder of voting stock of the member firm
    (B) is illegal
    (C) shall be approved according to NYSE rules in advance by a general partner/holder of voting stock
    (D) shall be approved in advance by a branch office manager according to NYSE rules

CORRECT ANSWERS TO SECURITIES BUSINESS PROCEDURES

Number in parenthesis, after answer, identifies number of reference source where information relating to the question and correct answer may be found.

1. D (3)	16. C (10)	31. A (1)	46. D (3)	61. A (1)
2. A (1)	17. A (10)	32. C (1)	47. C (1)	62. B (1)
3. A (1)	18. A (10)	33. D (1)	48. D (3)	63. D (1)
4. D (3)	19. A (10)	34. D (3)	49. D (3)	64. C (1)
5. D (3)	20. D (10)	35. A (1)	50. B (3)	65. B (1)
6. B (3)	21. C (3)	36. C (1)	51. C (3)	66. B (1)
7. A (3)	22. A (1)	37. A (3)	52. A (1)	67. A (1)
8. D (10)	23. B (1)	38. A (3)	53. B (1)	68. C (1)
9. A (10)	24. A (1)	39. B (3)	54. D (1)	69. A (3)
10. C (10)	25. A (1)	40. A (3)	55. C (1)	70. A (3)
11. A (10)	26. D (1)	41. D (3)	56. D (1)	71. A (3)
12. B (10)	27. A (1)	42. A (1)	57. D (1)	72. B (3)
13. D (10)	28. A (1)	43. A (3)	58. A (1)	73. D (3)
14. A (10)	29. B (1)	44. D (10)	59. C (1)	74. A (3)
15. A (10)	30. D (10)	45. A (3)	60. A (1)	75. A (1)

LIST OF REFERENCES

1. *New York Stock Exchange Constitution & Rules,* New York Stock Exchange, New York, N. Y.
2. *NASD Manual,* National Association of Securities Dealers, Washington, D. C.
3. *NASD Training Guide,* National Association of Securities Dealers, Washington, D. C.
4. *Fundamentals of the Money Market,* New York Stock Exchange, New York, N. Y.
5. *How to Invest on a Budget — MIP (Monthly Investment Plan),* New York Stock Exchange, New York, N. Y.
6. *The Interpretation of Financial Statements,* Graham & McGolrick — Harper & Row, Publishers, New York, N. Y.
7. *The Stock Market,* Leffler, Farwell — Ronald Press Company, New York, N. Y.
8. *Securities* — Volume 2, Second Edition; *Financial Planning and Mutual Funds,* Kalb, Voorhis & Co., New York, N. Y.
9. *Your Federal Income Tax,* Internal Revenue Service — Production Company, Scarborough, New York.
10. *Manual for Registered Representatives,* Association of Stock Exchange Firms (ASEF), New York, N. Y.
11. *American Stock Exchange Constitution,* American Stock Exchange, New York, N. Y.

ARCO PRACTICE ANSWER SHEET **5. Organized Exchanges**

USE THE SPECIAL PENCIL. MAKE GLOSSY BLACK MARKS.

1	A	B	C	D	26	A	B	C	D	51	A	B	C	D	76	A	B	C	D	101	A	B	C	D
2	A	B	C	D	27	A	B	C	D	52	A	B	C	D	77	A	B	C	D	102	A	B	C	D
3	A	B	C	D	28	A	B	C	D	53	A	B	C	D	78	A	B	C	D	103	A	B	C	D
4	A	B	C	D	29	A	B	C	D	54	A	B	C	D	79	A	B	C	D	104	A	B	C	D
5	A	B	C	D	30	A	B	C	D	55	A	B	C	D	80	A	B	C	D	105	A	B	C	D
6	A	B	C	D	31	A	B	C	D	56	A	B	C	D	81	A	B	C	D	106	A	B	C	D
7	A	B	C	D	32	A	B	C	D	57	A	B	C	D	82	A	B	C	D	107	A	B	C	D
8	A	B	C	D	33	A	B	C	D	58	A	B	C	D	83	A	B	C	D	108	A	B	C	D
9	A	B	C	D	34	A	B	C	D	59	A	B	C	D	84	A	B	C	D	109	A	B	C	D
10	A	B	C	D	35	A	B	C	D	60	A	B	C	D	85	A	B	C	D	110	A	B	C	D
11	A	B	C	D	36	A	B	C	D	61	A	B	C	D	86	A	B	C	D	111	A	B	C	D
12	A	B	C	D	37	A	B	C	D	62	A	B	C	D	87	A	B	C	D	112	A	B	C	D
13	A	B	C	D	38	A	B	C	D	63	A	B	C	D	88	A	B	C	D	113	A	B	C	D
14	A	B	C	D	39	A	B	C	D	64	A	B	C	D	89	A	B	C	D	114	A	B	C	D
15	A	B	C	D	40	A	B	C	D	65	A	B	C	D	90	A	B	C	D	115	A	B	C	D
16	A	B	C	D	41	A	B	C	D	66	A	B	C	D	91	A	B	C	D	116	A	B	C	D
17	A	B	C	D	42	A	B	C	D	67	A	B	C	D	92	A	B	C	D	117	A	B	C	D
18	A	B	C	D	43	A	B	C	D	68	A	B	C	D	93	A	B	C	D	118	A	B	C	D
19	A	B	C	D	44	A	B	C	D	69	A	B	C	D	94	A	B	C	D	119	A	B	C	D
20	A	B	C	D	45	A	B	C	D	70	A	B	C	D	95	A	B	C	D	120	A	B	C	D
21	A	B	C	D	46	A	B	C	D	71	A	B	C	D	96	A	B	C	D	121	A	B	C	D
22	A	B	C	D	47	A	B	C	D	72	A	B	C	D	97	A	B	C	D	122	A	B	C	D
23	A	B	C	D	48	A	B	C	D	73	A	B	C	D	98	A	B	C	D	123	A	B	C	D
24	A	B	C	D	49	A	B	C	D	74	A	B	C	D	99	A	B	C	D	124	A	B	C	D
25	A	B	C	D	50	A	B	C	D	75	A	B	C	D	100	A	B	C	D	125	A	B	C	D

5. Organized Exchanges

1. The NYSE was founded on

    (A) May 17, 1792 by 12 brokers
    (B) November 17, 1792 by 24 brokers
    (C) June 17, 1792 by 12 brokers
    (D) May 17, 1792 by 24 brokers

2. The body who has overall control of the member firms of the NYSE and their personnel is the

    (A) Board of Governors
    (B) Board of Trustees
    (C) SEC
    (D) Association of Stock Exchange Firms

3. The Board of Governors of the NYSE consists of

    (A) 12 members
    (B) 33 members
    (C) 23 members
    (D) 30 members

4. Membership on the NYSE Board of Governors has representatives from all of the following *except*:

    (A) allied members
    (B) the public
    (C) SEC
    (D) members

5. The Chairman of the Board of the NYSE is elected

    (A) annually by the membership of the Exchange
    (B) annually by the member firms
    (C) every 2 years by the membership of the Exchange
    (D) every 2 years by the member firms

6. The Chairman of the NYSE Board of Governors

    (A) may be a member of the public
    (B) may be a member or allied member
    (C) must be an allied member
    (D) must be a member of the Exchange

7. The President of the NYSE

    (A) is selected by the membership of the Exchange
    (B) is not a member of the NYSE Board of Governors
    (C) is a member of the NYSE Board of Governors
    (D) may be a member of the Exchange

8. The membership of the NYSE is

    (A) unlimited in number
    (B) fixed at 1375 memberships
    (C) fixed at 1366 memberships
    (D) fixed at 1366 memberships and allied memberships

9. The basic qualifications for membership on the NYSE as expressed in the constitution are

    (A) financial ability and 21 years of age
    (B) 21 years of age and U. S. citizen

(C) sponsorship by 2 other members
(D) completion of a qualification examination

10. Memberships on the NYSE are owned by

(A) member firms
(B) individuals
(C) the NYSE itself
(D) banks

11. The provision of the ABC arrangement would apply when a member's seat was

(A) purchased by the member's firm
(B) purchased by the applicant's own means
(C) received as a gift
(D) purchased through the member's direct borrowing at a bank

12. The auction market is conducted on the floor of the NYSE by

(A) staff employees of the NYSE
(B) members or allied members
(C) members or registered representatives
(D) members only

13. The member of the NYSE who exclusively trades for his own account is called a

(A) registered trader
(B) specialist
(C) commission house broker
(D) $2 broker

14. The member of the NYSE who performs the function of a broker's broker is the

(A) $2 broker
(B) commission house broker
(C) old lot "broker"
(D) specialist

15. The member who executes the orders for the clients of the firm with which he is associated is called a

(A) registered trader
(B) odd lot dealer
(C) commission house broker
(D) specialist

16. The member of the NYSE who consistently performs both broker and dealer functions is the

(A) odd lot member
(B) commission house member
(C) registered trader
(D) specialist

17. The specialist's prime function as a dealer is to

(A) maintain an orderly market in the stocks in which he is the specialist
(B) execute orders left with him by other members
(C) buy and sell shares in those stocks he feels look attractive for trading
(D) assemble small orders into larger round lot orders for trading

18. The unit of trading in stocks on the floor of the NYSE, with certain exceptions, is

(A) 10 shares
(B) 1,000 shares
(C) 100 shares
(D) the number of shares available at that moment

19. The minimum variation for stocks above one dollar per share is

(A) 1/32
(B) ¼
(C) ⅛
(D) 15 cents

20. A stock listed on the NYSE trades

(A) wherever buyers and sellers get together
(B) at several different posts
(C) at one specific post only
(D) between specialists for that issue

21. The quote at any moment of time in a stock equals the

(A) highest bid and lowest offer
(B) lowest bid and highest offer
(C) last sale price of the stock
(D) last purchase price of the stock

22. On the NYSE, there is competition among

 (A) both buyers and sellers of any stock
 (B) the sellers in a stock only
 (C) the buyers in a stock only
 (D) specialists in the stock

23. In the auction market, priority is defined as

 (A) price of the order
 (B) size of the order to be executed
 (C) time in the crowd at the post
 (D) flip of a coin to determine who trades

24. If all bidders enter the crowd simultaneously, the member with the largest order has

 (A) priority
 (B) precedence
 (C) parity
 (D) par

25. "Matched and lost" would have represented a situation of

 (A) par
 (B) priority
 (C) parity
 (D) precedence

26. The phraseology used in connection with accepting an offer of stock is

 (A) Hold it for me
 (B) "Sold"
 (C) DK
 (D) "Take it"

27. The phraseology 20 to ½, 200-500 represents

 (A) quotation in a stock
 (B) range of the stock
 (C) execution of a trade in a stock
 (D) quote and size of a stock

28. A commission house member has your order to sell T short at the market. As he enters the crowd, transactions occur at 52⅛, 52, 51¾, 51⅞. Your order could be offered at

 (A) 52
 (B) 51¾
 (C) 51⅞
 (D) 52⅛

29. 1,000 shares of MXR are offered for sale. Simultaneous bid orders are placed in the crowd by brokers A-600 shares, B-300, C-200, D-100, and E-100. Stock is taken by

 (A) A-600; B-300; C, D, and E match
 (B) A-600; B-300; C and D match
 (C) A-600; B-300; C-100
 (D) A-600; B-300; D-10

30. In the auction market the following bids and offers stand on the floor. A arrived in the crowd and wants 100 shares. He is followed by B for 200 shares, C 400 shares, D 300 shares and E 500 shares. F offers 1,000 shares. It is taken by

 (A) A-100 shares, E-500 shares, C-400 shares
 (B) A-100 shares; E-500 shares; and a match by B, C, and D
 (C) E-500 shares; C-400 shares; and a match by A, B, and D
 (D) A-100 shares, B-200 shares, D-300 shares, and C-400 shares in that order

31. In order to cross stock on the floor the quote for that stock must have a minimum variation of

 (A) ½
 (B) ⅛
 (C) ⅜
 (D) ¼

32. A stop order to buy a security would be placed

 (A) below the then current market
 (B) above the then current market
 (C) at the then current market
 (D) either above or below the then current market

33. A stop order to sell 75 OEX at 32 will be executed

 (A) 32⅛
 (B) 32
 (C) 31⅞

(D) at a price that can not be determined from this information

34. A stop order is

(A) a guarantee of the price at which the order is entered
(B) not a guarantee of a specific price
(C) a guarantee of at least the price at which the order was entered
(D) a guarantee of the *maximum* of the price at which the order was entered

35. The two parties to stopping stock on the floor of the Exchange are the

(A) registered trader and the odd lot dealer
(B) commission house broker and odd lot dealer
(C) registered trader and the specialist
(D) commission house broker and specialist

36. Stopping stock is

(A) when trading is suspended in an issue
(B) not a guarantee of a specific price
(C) a guarantee of at least the price of the stop
(D) done off the floor of the NYSE

37. A client who receives an erroneous report of a trade on the NYSE

(A) must accept the actual, true execution price
(B) may hold the member firm to that trade
(C) may have the trade "adjusted" through an error account
(D) can cancel the trade as the firm made a mistake

38. You see a print on the tape of stock at the price of a limit order you had entered. However, you receive no confirmation of an execution. A reason for this could be

(A) basis order
(B) par
(C) not held order
(D) stock ahead

39. Clients on regular way trades must deliver the securities no later than the

(A) 5th business day after trade date
(B) 5th calendar day after trade date
(C) 7th calendar day after trade date
(D) 7th business day after trade date

40. Trades made in stocks for cash settle the

(A) 5th business day
(B) next business day
(C) 4th business day
(D) same day

41. The type of bonds that trade on the NYSE are

(A) revenues
(B) general obligations
(C) corporates
(D) none: only stocks trade on the NYSE

42. For a listed bond, which order must be sent to the floor?

(A) order for 9 bonds or less
(B) order for 10 bonds or more
(C) all orders for corporate bonds
(D) no orders for corporate bonds

43. Cabinet securities could include

(A) bonds and some 10 share unit stocks
(B) all bonds traded on the NYSE
(C) all preferred stocks traded on NYSE
(D) any listed common stock

44. Which of the following orders may not be placed in the cabinets for securities of the NYSE?

(A) month orders
(B) week orders
(C) stop orders
(D) G.T.C. orders

45. The fee which the odd lot dealer charges on a public order is called

(A) a mark up
(B) a commission

(C) the differential
(D) the sales charge

46. Odd lot orders are executed against the

(A) opening round lot purchase
(B) last round lot purchase
(C) last round lot sale
(D) closing round lot purchase

47. The differential on an odd lot trade on the NYSE of a stock whose market price is $40 per share is

(A) ¼
(B) ⅛
(C) ⅜
(D) ½

48. A client wants to sell 40 shares of CA at the market. Round lot sales occur at 39, 39⅛, 39⅛ just before the order is received by the odd lot dealer. The next round lot is executed at 39¼. The client obtains

(A) 39
(B) 39¼
(C) 39⅛
(D) 39⅜

49. HO sells at 45⅛ just before a short odd lot market order reaches the dealer on the NYSE. Sales then occur at 45, 45, 44⅞, 45. The odd lot would be confirmed at

(A) 44¾
(B) 45
(C) 45⅛
(D) 44⅞

50. An odd lot order is entered to sell 35 OXY at 48¼ long. The stock trades at 48¼ and then 49¼. The customer receives

(A) 49
(B) 48¼
(C) 49¼
(D) 49⅛

51. On which of the following sequences of trades could a short sale be made?

(A) 50⅛, 50⅛, 50⅛, 50
(B) 50⅛, 50⅛, 50, 49⅞
(C) 50, 50⅛, 50⅛, 50
(D) 50¼, 50⅛, 50⅛, 50

52. A zero minus tick is illustrated by which sequence?

(A) 50¼, 50⅛, 50⅛, 50
(B) 50, 50⅛, 50⅛, 50
(C) 50⅛, 50⅛, 50, 49⅞
(D) 50⅛, 50⅛, 50⅛, 50

53. A short sale is the

(A) sale of stock in the hope it will go down
(B) sale of stock in the hope it will go up
(C) purchase of stock in the hope it will go up
(D) purchase of stock in the hope it will go down

54. Short selling regulations come from the

(A) NASD only
(B) Securities Act of 1933
(C) NYSE only
(D) NYSE and SEC

55. Prints on the NYSE tape represent

(A) the round and odd lot sales of each stock
(B) the buys and sells in each stock
(C) round lot trades in each stock
(D) selective round lot trades in listed stocks

56. The print on the tape IBM 4s325 means

(A) 4 shares of IBM sold at 325
(B) 400 shares of IBM sold at 325
(C) 40 shares of IBM sold at 325
(D) 4,000 shares of IBM sold at 325

57. Which of the following trades would show the number of shares in full on the tape?

(A) 100
(B) 900
(C) 500
(D) 1,500

58. A block trading method that prints on the tape ahead of time soliciting orders is the

    (A) specialist offer
    (B) special offer
    (C) exchange distribution
    (D) secondary distribution

59. Which of the following block trading methods is a part of the auction procedure?

    (A) special offer
    (B) secondary distribution
    (C) specialist offer
    (D) exchange distribution

60. The type of block trade that prints on the tape when it is crossed in the then current market is

    (A) special bid
    (B) special offer
    (C) an exchange acquisition
    (D) secondary distribution

61. The block trade method which would never appear on the tape, neither before nor after the trade, is the

    (A) special bid
    (B) specialist bid
    (C) secondary distribution
    (D) exchange distribution

62. Securities that can be bought through MIP are

    (A) mutual funds
    (B) publicly owned stocks
    (C) publicly owned stocks or bonds
    (D) common stock listed on the NYSE

63. The prime feature of MIP is

    (A) dollar cost averaging
    (B) averaging the dollar
    (C) installment buying
    (D) deferred income

64. The minimum amount that can be put in an MIP plan is

    (A) $50 per month
    (B) $40 per month
    (C) $40 per quarter
    (D) $50 per quarter

65. Under an MIP plan, it is

    (A) possible to vote if you hold 100 shares or more
    (B) possible to vote all full shares
    (C) not possible to vote at all
    (D) not possible to vote unless the issue affects MIP shareholders interest

66. For listing stock, the NYSE would look for demonstrated earnings power of

    (A) any year of $2 million pre-tax earnings over the last 5 years
    (B) $2 million pre-tax earnings over the last 3 years
    (C) $2.5 million pre-tax for the previous year and 2 years of $2 million pre-tax earnings before that
    (D) $1 million pre-tax for the last 3 years

67. To apply for listing on the NYSE, a company must have at least

    (A) 1 million shares outstanding with 800,000 in public hands
    (B) 10 million shares outstanding with 800,000 in public hands
    (C) 5 million shares outstanding with 2.5 million in public hands
    (D) 3 million shares outstanding with 1 million in public hands

68. The minimum number of round lot holders looked for in listing a stock on the NYSE is

    (A) 2,500
    (B) 1,500
    (C) 2,000
    (D) 1,800

69. The procedures for delisting a stock from the NYSE

    (A) provide guidelines to be reviewed if a stock falls to those levels
    (B) are inflexible and call for immediate delisting of issues that fall below the accepted levels

(C) are unwritten
(D) are controlled by the SEC

70. Securities that settle through Stock Clearing Corporation are

(A) municipal securities
(B) OTC securities
(C) NYSE listed trades
(D) government securities

71. The Stock Clearing Corporation is a

(A) wholly owned subsidiary of the ASEF
(B) trade association
(C) branch of the SEC
(D) wholly owned subsidiary of the NYSE

72. The central certificate service is meant to

(A) cut down the physical delivery of securities between member firms
(B) reduce the time of transfer of securities
(C) increase the client's holding of stock in his own name
(D) increase the "fails" between firms

73. The NYSE requires proxies to be solicited

(A) for all listed stocks and bonds
(B) for all listed common bonds
(C) for all listed common stocks
(D) only if the corporation desires

74. The so-called 10 day rule in connection with proxies means

(A) the member firm may vote shares if the shareholder has not replied within 10 days of the meeting date
(B) the member firm may vote shares if the shareholder has not replied within 10 days of the record date.
(C) all votes are void unless cast 10 days before meeting date
(D) all votes are void unless cast 10 days before record date

75. The member firm who is shown on the books of the corporation as the owner of stock is called the

(A) rightful owner.
(B) street name owner
(C) beneficial owner
(D) holder of record

76. The "true" owner of a street name certificate is called the

(A) trustee
(B) holder of record
(C) beneficial owner
(D) nominee

77. In proxy contests, member firms may vote street name certificates

(A) only as specifically authorized by the beneficial owner
(B) only as specifically authorized by the holder of record
(C) in any way they desire
(D) in accord with management of the companies recommendations

78. All of the following are provisions of the Securities Exchange Act of 1934 *except:*

(A) delivery of prospectus requirement
(B) creation of the SEC
(C) setting up borrowing restrictions
(D) permitting the regulation of the OTC markets

79. Among the objectives of the NYSE as expressed in its constitution is

(A) furnishing rooms to members for transacting business
(B) settling disputes through arbitration
(C) establishing disciplinary procedures
(D) establishing trading procedures

80. Rules of the NYSE apply directly to

(A) RR's of a member firm
(B) members only
(C) member and/or allied members
(D) all personnel employed by a member firm

81. Arbitration proceedings can be brought by

(A) a member firm; an RR; a member of the public
(B) a member firm
(C) an RR
(D) a member of the public

82. To be heard at arbitration, a controversy must

(A) arise out of the business of the member
(B) involve two member firms
(C) involve two RR's
(D) involve a member of the public

83. A decision of a Board of Arbitration is made by

(A) unanimous vote
(B) ⅔ vote
(C) ¾ vote
(D) majority vote

84. Which of the following categories of activities is *not* included in the NYSE definition of an RR?

(A) occasional entry of an order by a secretary
(B) handling investment advisory accounts on a fee basis
(C) international securities arbitration activities
(D) supervision of the foreign business of the firm

85. For an individual who has no previous securities experience to become fully registered with a NYSE member firm requires

(A) seven months training
(B) six months training
(C) three months training
(D) five months training

86. Which of the following would *not* be a factor in determining the acceptability of a candidate for registration with an NYSE firm?

(A) age
(B) U. S. citizenship
(C) past business background
(D) financial responsibilities

87. A release from all liability in connection with furnishing information as to the character, ability, business activities and reputation is given by an RR

(A) to the NYSE when he signs his RE-1 form
(B) to his member firm as soon as he accepts employment
(C) to the SEC by his accepting employment in the highly regulated securities industry
(D) in no cases as this would be illegal

88. A candidate for registration with a NYSE member firm indicates that he

(A) has read the NYSE Constitution and Rules
(B) will report any change in his firm's compensation procedures to the NYSE
(C) will obtain NYSE approval of all outside activities relating to the securities business in which he may engage
(D) is always going to remain a U. S. citizen

89. With the prior written consent of the Exchange, an RR can

(A) guarantee the payment of a debt balance in a customer's account to his employer
(B) guarantee the payment of a debit balance in an account to a customer
(C) guarantee the payment of a loss in an account to a customer
(D) share in the losses sustained in a customer's account

90. An RR with a NYSE member firm may *not* have a securities account with

(A) another NYSE member firm
(B) a bank
(C) a non-NYSE member firm
(D) his own firm

91. If an RR is arrested or becomes involved in litigation after registration, he

(A) must promptly notify the NYSE

(B) must promptly notify the SEC
(C) need do nothing unless the litigation or arrest arose out of the securities business
(D) is forced to terminate his employment with a member firm

92. The candidate for registration agrees to remain subject to NYSE jurisdiction if notified of an inquiry being in process within

(A) 60 days following termination with the member firm
(B) 10 days following termination with the member firm
(C) 20 days following termination with the member firm
(D) 30 days following termination with the member firm

93. An RR commits himself to appear before a hearing, give evidence and produce any records requested in connection with an inquiry by the NYSE

(A) by his signing the RE-4 form
(B) by his signing the RE-1 form
(C) by his accepting employment with a member firm
(D) in no cases as this would violate his civil rights

94. An RR can become the director of what number of corporations, not in the securities business, without NYSE approval?

(A) none
(B) up to 4
(C) up to 5
(D) up to 3

95. Which of the following activities would require NYSE prior approval?

(A) teaching a course in architecture in a community college in the evenings
(B) giving a series of lectures on investments to the local PTA group
(C) writing an article on mutual funds for the Investment Dealers Digest
(D) appearing on a panel show on TV to discuss investment banking activities

96. While on a leave of absence, an RR

(A) can be gone for up to 24 months
(B) can receive compensation from the firm
(C) can not engage in another business
(D) can transact occasional business from the firm's office

97. An RR can be compensated on his own production or from accounts in which he has personal interest up to 10% of total commission on all

(A) other accounts accredited to him on an annual basis
(B) other accounts accredited to him on a monthly basis
(C) accounts accredited to him on an annual basis
(D) accounts accredited to him on a monthly basis

98. The maximum gratuity an employee of a member firm may receive is

(A) $25 per person per year
(B) $25 from all clients per year
(C) $50 from all clients per year
(D) $50 per person per year

99. The NYSE requires records of gratuities to be maintained for at least

(A) 1 year
(B) 2 years
(C) 3 years
(D) 5 years

100. Rule 405 of the NYSE requires that all accounts be "approved promptly" by

(A) a general partner of the member firm
(B) the branch office manager concerned
(C) the RR who handles the account
(D) the new account department of the firm

101. The responsibility to "Know Your Customer" is that of the

(A) RR, branch office manager and general partner

(B) RR only
(C) RR and branch office manager only
(D) branch office manager and general partner alone

102. Rule 405 requires that all new accounts must be approved by

(A) the RR
(B) a general partner of the firm
(C) the branch office manager
(D) the customer's attorney

103. An account can be designated by a symbol on the books of the member firm

(A) upon written request of a client and his attesting that the securities are his
(B) upon oral request of a client and his attesting that the securities are his
(C) under no circumstances
(D) if prior consent of the NYSE is obtained

104. A securities account for a corporation

(A) requires information as to who can make commitments for the corporation
(B) is illegal
(C) always requires counsel assistance before opening
(D) always requires NYSE approval before accepting

105. A general partner of one member firm may

(A) have no account with another member firm without prior written consent of another general partner
(B) *never* have a personal account at another member firm
(C) have an account at another member firm if he desires without any special procedures
(D) have an account at another member firm *only* with NYSE approval

106. An occupation that requires duplicates of transactions to be sent to the account's employer is an employee of

(A) the NYSE
(B) a bank
(C) a member firm
(D) the ASEF

107. Prior written consent to open a margin account would be required for

(A) a city employee
(B) a bank guard
(C) a trust officer of a local bank
(D) an FBI agent

108. Prior written consent is required for all of the following accounts for an employee of a member firm who opens an account at another member firm except

(A) a short account
(B) a cash account
(C) a margin account
(D) an MIP account

109. Orders in a discretionary account must be approved

(A) on the day entered by a general partner
(B) before being entered by a general partner
(C) before being entered by the resident manager
(D) on the day entered by the resident manager

110. Before entering orders in a discretionary account, prior written authorization must be obtained from

(A) the branch office manager
(B) the customer
(C) a general partner
(D) the NYSE

111. NYSE rules require that statements of accounts be sent to customers having active accounts

(A) after each trade
(B) at least monthly
(C) at least semi-annually
(D) at least quarterly

112. Records of every NYSE order sent to the floor for execution shall be preserved for

(A) 2 years
(B) 6 years
(C) 1 year
(D) 3 years

113. Odd lot orders may be bunched into a round lot order

(A) with the prior approval of the customers involved
(B) any time the firm desires
(C) under *no* circumstances
(D) only with NYSE approval

114. The NYSE requires each member firm to have a surprise audit by independent public accountants at least once every

(A) two years
(B) six months
(C) quarter
(D) year

115. After completion of the outside audit a copy of the results shall be sent by the auditor to the member firm and the

(A) NASD
(B) NYSE
(C) SEC
(D) state regulatory body

116. The NYSE requires that a financial statement must be made available upon request to

(A) any member of the public
(B) any prospective client
(C) any customer
(D) all other member firms

117. The financial statement that must be made available upon request is the member firm's

(A) statement of retained earnings
(B) profit and loss statement
(C) balance sheet and profit and loss statement
(D) balance sheet

118. The NYSE requires member firms advertising to be

(A) filed before use
(B) submitted for approval after use
(C) submitted for approval before use
(D) filed after use

119. According to the NYSE, advertisements concerning new offices or RR's being approved are

(A) routine and do not require special advertisement approval
(B) routine and do require special advertisement approval
(C) subject to the general rules of all advertisement by NYSE firms
(D) not to be the subject of ads

120. Research reports for general distribution to the public shall be approved in all cases by a

(A) supervisory analyst
(B) director of research
(C) allied member
(D) member

121. Copies of all research reports shall show the name of the person who prepared the report and be retained for

(A) 4 years
(B) 2 years
(C) 1 year
(D) 3 years

122. According to NYSE rules, market letters, sales literature or research reports must disclose if

(A) the firm makes a market in the issue
(B) the firm underwrote the issue 10 years ago
(C) a partner holds a directorship in the firm
(D) a partner of the firm bought or sold any shares of the issue in the past 10 days

123. One of the differences between the American Stock Exchange and the NYSE is

(A) handling of odd lot orders
(B) market and limit order procedures
(C) specialist system
(D) commission charged on transactions

124. An order which is not acceptable on the AMEX is

(A) an odd lot short sale
(B) an odd lot stop order
(C) a round lot short sale
(D) a round lot stop order

125. An example of a dual listing of a stock would be a stock listed on the NYSE as well as on the

(A) Midwest Stock Exchange
(B) AMEX
(C) National Stock Exchange
(D) Over-the-Counter-Market

CORRECT ANSWERS TO ORGANIZED EXCHANGES

Number in parenthesis, after answer, identifies number of reference source where information relating to the question and correct answer may be found.

1. D (7)
2. A (1)
3. B (1)
4. C (1)
5. A (1)
6. D (1)
7. C (1)
8. C (1)
9. B (1)
10. B (1)
11. A (1)
12. D (1)
13. A (7)
14. A (7)
15. C (7)
16. D (7)
17. A (7)
18. C (1)
19. C (1)
20. C (1)
21. A (1)
22. A (1)
23. C (1)
24. B (1)
25. C (1)
26. D (1)
27. D (1)
28. C (1)
29. A (1)
30. A (1)
31. D (1)
32. B (1)
33. D (1)
34. B (1)
35. D (1)
36. C (1)
37. A (1)
38. D (1)
39. A (1)
40. D (1)
41. C (1)
42. A (1)
43. A (1)
44. C (1)
45. C (1)
46. C (1)
47. B (1)
48. C (1)
49. D (1)
50. D (1)
51. C (1)
52. A (1)
53. A (1)
54. D (1)
55. C (1)
56. B (1)
57. D (1)
58. B (1)
59. D (1)
60. C (1)
61. B (1)
62. D (5)
63. A (5)
64. C (5)
65. B (5)
66. C (1)
67. A (1)
68. D (1)
69. A (1)
70. C (1)
71. D (1)
72. A (1)
73. C (1)
74. A (1)
75. D (1)
76. C (1)
77. A (1)
78. A (3)
79. A (1)
80. C (1)
81. A (1)
82. A (1)
83. D (1)
84. A (1)
85. C (1)
86. B (1)
87. A (1)
88. A (1)
89. A (1)
90. C (1)
91. A (1)
92. D (1)
93. B (1)
94. D (1)
95. A (1)
96. C (1)
97. A (1)
98. A (1)
99. C (1)
100. A (1)
101. A (1)
102. B (1)
103. A (1)
104. A (10)
105. A (1)
106. C (1)
107. B (1)
108. D (1)
109. A (1)
110. B (1)
111. D (1)
112. D (1)
113. A (1)
114. D (1)
115. B (1)
116. C (1)
117. D (1)
118. C (1)
119. A (1)
120. A (1)
121. D (1)
122. A (1)
123. A (11)
124. D (11)
125. A (7)

LIST OF REFERENCES

1. *New York Stock Exchange Constitution & Rules,* New York Stock Exchange, New York, N. Y.
2. *NASD Manual,* National Association of Securities Dealers, Washington, D. C.
3. *NASD Training Guide,* National Association of Securities Dealers, Washington, D. C.
4. *Fundamentals of the Money Market,* New York Stock Exchange, New York, N. Y.
5. *How to Invest on a Budget — MIP (Monthly Investment Plan),* New York Stock Exchange, New York, N. Y.
6. *The Interpretation of Financial Statements,* Graham & McGolrick — Harper & Row, Publishers, New York, N. Y.
7. *The Stock Market,* Leffler, Farwell — Ronald Press Company, New York, N. Y.
8. *Securities* — Volume 2, Second Edition; *Financial Planning and Mutual Funds,* Kalb, Voorhis & Co., New York, N. Y.
9. *Your Federal Income Tax,* Internal Revenue Service — Production Company, Scarborough, New York.
10. *Manual for Registered Representatives,* Association of Stock Exchange Firms (ASEF), New York, N. Y.
11. *American Stock Exchange Constitution,* American Stock Exchange, New York, N. Y.

ARCO PRACTICE ANSWER SHEET

6. Over-the-Counter-Market and the NASD

USE THE SPECIAL PENCIL. MAKE GLOSSY BLACK MARKS.

1	A	B	C	D	26	A	B	C	D	51	A	B	C	D
2	A	B	C	D	27	A	B	C	D	52	A	B	C	D
3	A	B	C	D	28	A	B	C	D	53	A	B	C	D
4	A	B	C	D	29	A	B	C	D	54	A	B	C	D
5	A	B	C	D	30	A	B	C	D	55	A	B	C	D
6	A	B	C	D	31	A	B	C	D	56	A	B	C	D
7	A	B	C	D	32	A	B	C	D	57	A	B	C	D
8	A	B	C	D	33	A	B	C	D	58	A	B	C	D
9	A	B	C	D	34	A	B	C	D	59	A	B	C	D
10	A	B	C	D	35	A	B	C	D	60	A	B	C	D
11	A	B	C	D	36	A	B	C	D	61	A	B	C	D
12	A	B	C	D	37	A	B	C	D	62	A	B	C	D
13	A	B	C	D	38	A	B	C	D	63	A	B	C	D
14	A	B	C	D	39	A	B	C	D	64	A	B	C	D
15	A	B	C	D	40	A	B	C	D	65	A	B	C	D
16	A	B	C	D	41	A	B	C	D	66	A	B	C	D
17	A	B	C	D	42	A	B	C	D	67	A	B	C	D
18	A	B	C	D	43	A	B	C	D	68	A	B	C	D
19	A	B	C	D	44	A	B	C	D	69	A	B	C	D
20	A	B	C	D	45	A	B	C	D	70	A	B	C	D
21	A	B	C	D	46	A	B	C	D	71	A	B	C	D
22	A	B	C	D	47	A	B	C	D	72	A	B	C	D
23	A	B	C	D	48	A	B	C	D	73	A	B	C	D
24	A	B	C	D	49	A	B	C	D	74	A	B	C	D
25	A	B	C	D	50	A	B	C	D	75	A	B	C	D

6. Over-the-Counter-Market and the NASD

1. The OTC is characterized by being

   (A) a negotiated market
   (B) a commission *only* market
   (C) an auction market
   (D) a centralized market

2. A firm which makes a market in a security acts as a

   (A) broker
   (B) dealer
   (C) underwriter
   (D) syndicator

3. Typically a dealer in the OTC market receives his compensation from a

   (A) lift up
   (B) commission
   (C) mark up
   (D) differential

4. When a listed stock trades over-the-counter, it is said to trade in the

   (A) prime market
   (B) third market
   (C) auction market
   (D) secondary market

5. The information shown in newspapers concerning OTC stocks represents

   (A). quotations as of a specific time
   (B) actual prices as of a specific time
   (C) actual trades as of a specific time
   (D) range of trading in the stock that day

6. OTC quotations supplied in newspapers by the NASD are bids and offers

   (A) quoted by OTC dealers to each other
   (B) quoted by OTC dealers to the public
   (C) at which trades were made to the public
   (D) at which trades were made among OTC dealers

7. The difference between the bid and asked quotation of an OTC stock is the

   (A) mark up
   (B) spread
   (C) sales charge
   (D) differential

8. Information as to who is making a market in any particular OTC stock is found by consulting

   (A) the pink sheets
   (B) the stock tape
   (C) Dow Jones Broad Tape
   (D) Standard & Poor's OTC reports

9. Which of the following represents a firm quote?

   (A) 40 to ¼

(B) last I heard was 35-36
(C) the sheets show 43-43¼
(D) 40-41, subject

10. The contract that permits a person to purchase 100 shares of a stock at a specific price through a specific date is called a

(A) put option
(B) call option
(C) confirmation
(D) letter of intent

11. The type of banker who assists in obtaining capital for industry is called

(A) an investment banker
(B) a commercial banker
(C) a savings and loan banker
(D) a credit banker

12. An offering of securities never before offered to the public is called

(A) a primary distribution
(B) a secondary distribution
(C) a give up distribution
(D) an exchange distribution

13. In investment banking the firm in charge of a syndicate is called the

(A) mafia
(B) managing underwriting
(C) selling group
(D) market maker

14. When several investment bankers join together in an underwriting with liability they have formed

(A) an association
(B) a selling group
(C) a registration group
(D) a syndicate

15. After a new issue has been placed in registration, there is a "cooling period" of a minimum of

(A) 30 days
(B) 2 weeks
(C) 20 days
(D) 45 days

16. Toward the end of the cooling period, the underwriters, officers of the corporation and the legal staff have a meeting called a

(A) private placement meeting
(B) registration meeting
(C) due diligence meeting
(D) prospectus meeting

17. A type of security issue sold to the underwriters under competitive bidding procedures would be

(A) mutual funds
(B) public utility or railroad securities
(C) a new industrial issue
(D) a secondary distribution

18. Under competitive bidding procedures, the underwriting goes to the

(A) selling group submitting the highest interest bid
(B) syndicate submitting the lowest interest bid
(C) selling group submitting the lowest interest bid
(D) syndicate submitting the highest interest bid

19. A "hot issue" underwriting is one where

(A) the price of the issue immediately drops
(B) supply exceeds demand
(C) there is no underwriter of the issue, and the firm has its own money "on the firing line."
(D) demand exceeds supply

20. One of the members of an underwriting syndicate purchases shares of the issue at or below the public offering price while sales are still being made at the public offering price. This is called

(A) participation
(B) fraud
(C) manipulation
(D) stabilization

21. The procedure of paying an investment banker for advice rather than underwriting of an issue is most typical of a

    (A) private placement
    (B) best effort underwriting
    (C) firm underwriting
    (D) secondary distribution

22. The raising of capital through the direct sale of securities to a financial institution, such as an insurance company, by a corporation is called

    (A) a private placement
    (B) a direct underwriting
    (C) a secondary distribution
    (D) an exchange distribution

23. The procedures concerning distribution of securities are covered by the federal law enacted in

    (A) 1933
    (B) 1934
    (C) 1938
    (D) 1940

24. The publication given to a prospective purchase of a new issue which *does not* include the price is called the

    (A) registration statement
    (B) prospectus
    (C) red herring
    (D) confirmation

25. Every person who receives a preliminary prospectus must also receive

    (A) a confirmation
    (B) a final prospectus
    (C) his desired number of shares of stock
    (D) a registration statement

26. In connection with an issue in registration, an RR would be correct in taking

    (A) indications of interest from clients
    (B) firm orders from clients
    (C) deposits on orders from clients
    (D) sell orders from clients

27. The one item that must be given to every purchaser of a new issue according to the Securities Act of 1933 is a

    (A) buy in
    (B) statement of account
    (C) prospectus
    (D) sell out

28. The so-called exemption from registration under the 1933 Act is called

    (A) Reg. B
    (B) Reg. A
    (C) Reg. T
    (D) Reg. U

29. This exemption from registration covers issues in the dollar amount of

    (A) $250,000 or less
    (B) $100,000 or less
    (C) $300,000 or less
    (D) $500,000 or less

30. The NASD came into being through the provisions of the

    (A) Securities Exchange Act of 1934
    (B) Investment Companies Act of 1940
    (C) Securities Act of 1933
    (D) Maloncy Act of 1938

31. Which of the following is *not* a purpose of the NASD as stated in its certificate of incorporation

    (A) to adopt and administrate rules for commodity trading
    (B) to promote observance of federal and state securities laws
    (C) to enforce rules of fair practice
    (D) to promote self-discipline among members

32. Membership in the NASD is open to broker-dealers transacting investment banking or securities business located in

    (A) United States
    (B) England
    (C) Japan
    (D) Mexico

33. Which of the following is *not* eligible for membership in the NASD?

(A) an investment banker
(B) an NYSE member firm who makes OTC markets
(C) a mutual fund retailer
(D) a commercial bank

34. A general partner or officer registered with an NASD member firm is called

(A) a principal
(B) an allied member
(C) an associate member
(D) a member

35. Unlike the NYSE, the NASD does not have

(A) a qualification exam
(B) a training period for registration
(C) a registration requirement
(D) disciplinary procedures for registered personnel

36. Resignations of members from the NASD take effect

(A) 90 days after receipt of notice by the NASD
(B) 60 days after receipt of notice by the NASD
(C) 30 days after receipt of notice by the NASD
(D) immediately upon receipt of notice by the NASD

37. The NASD is divided for administrative purposes into

(A) 10 districts
(B) 20 districts
(C) 12 districts
(D) 13 districts

38. Like the NYSE, the NASD is governed by a Board of Governors. The NASD's Board consists of

(A) 30 members
(B) 33 members
(C) 23 members
(D) 20 members

39. The representatives of the NASD Board who are elected by the Board rather than the membership are the

(A) president and the governor at large
(B) representatives of the public
(C) president and the representative of the public
(D) governor at large and the representative of the public

40. Members of the NASD Board of Governors are elected for a term of

(A) 2 years
(B) 3 years
(C) 4 years
(D) 1 year

41. The NASD is administered locally through

(A) the board of trustees
(B) the executive committee
(C) the regional committee
(D) the district committee

42. The NASD permits its name to be used in any of the following methods *except*:

(A) as a guarantee of the members business ethics
(B) as a matter of recognition in trade, directories, or business listings
(C) on the door or entranceway of the members principal office
(D) in institutional print advertising

43. The regulations which set business standards for members of the NASD are the

(A) by-laws
(B) rules of fair practice
(C) uniform practice code
(D) trade complaint procedures

44. The rules of fair practice apply to

(A) all members and persons associated with a member
(B) only the member firm
(C) only principals of the member firm
(D) any individual who is registered with an NYSE firm

45. The NASD requires that advertisements used by member firms be

    (A) filed for review within 5 business days of use
    (B) approved before use by the local NASD office
    (C) approved before use by the National NASD office
    (D) filed for review before use

46. Sales of a hot issue to banks for undisclosed principals

    (A) is illegal
    (B) is not covered by the NASD rules
    (C) is acceptable procedure and the member has no additional responsibility
    (D) does not relieve a member of its responsibility to insure a public distribution

47. Husband or wife, brother or sister, or in-laws are all included in the

    (A) NASD definition of immediate family
    (B) NYSE definition of immediate family
    (C) NYSE definition of insiders
    (D) NASD definition of insiders

48. If a client's account shows a practice of purchasing mainly "hot issues"

    (A) this means the account should continue to receive new issues
    (B) this means the account is acceptable
    (C) this is not considered a normal investment practice in the eyes of the NASD
    (D) it is ignored by the NASD

49. The regulatory organization which has a "suitability rule" is the

    (A) ASEF
    (B) NYSE
    (C) SEC
    (D) NASD

50. Excessive activity in a customer's account is called

    (A) burning
    (B) churning
    (C) speculation
    (D) expectation

51. Executing unauthorized transcriptions in any account is

    (A) fraudulent activity according to the NASD rules
    (B) common business practice for an RR
    (C) illegal under NYSE Rules, but not covered by the NASD's Rules
    (D) permitted by the NASD as long as the client accepts the confirmation

52. The NASD rules of fair practice state that charges for services performed for clients shall be

    (A) reasonable and not unfairly discriminatory between clients
    (B) reasonable and the same for all clients
    (C) free to the client and absorbed by the member firm
    (D) left entirely to the member firm to charge anything they see fit

53. The NASD has

    (A) a maximum commission schedule
    (B) a minimum commission schedule
    (C) no specific commission schedule
    (D) a 5% commission schedule

54. Principal transactions must be effected at

    (A) a reasonable commission
    (B) 5% over market price
    (C) 5% over cost price
    (D) a fair price

55. The mark up is applied to the

    (A) then current offer price
    (B) then current bid price
    (C) cost price of the security
    (D) prime market maker's quote.

56. The purchase by an NASD firm of securities from a client at a net price is

    (A) illegal
    (B) done at mark up from market

(C) done at mark down from market
(D) done plus commission

57. The NASD mark up policy is appropriate to be considered for
(A) a riskless trade
(B) a mutual fund purchase
(C) an issue sold by prospectus
(D) an agency trade

58. The NASD says that nominal quotations
(A) are unfair and unreasonable and a bad business practice
(B) are illegal
(C) are acceptable for transacting trades
(D) must be clearly stated as such

59. The NASD says that discretionary orders shall be
(A) approved promptly in writing
(B) unacceptable for any firm
(C) approved on the day entered
(D) approved before execution

60. The pledging of customers' securities as collateral for loans by the member firm is called
(A) a call loan
(B) rehypothecation
(C) fraud
(D) hypothecation

61. With the prior written consent of each client, securities of one client can be comingled with securities of
(A) other clients
(B) the partners
(C) the firm
(D) RR's of the firm

62. Bulk segregation of clients' securities physically separates the stocks by
(A) issue with a tab on each certificate to show ownership
(B) client with a list to show his holdings
(C) issue with a list in front to show ownership
(D) putting each certificate in an envelope showing the owner's name

63. The NASD requires that a separate file of all written complaints received from clients be maintained at
(A) the home office
(B) every branch office
(C) every office of supervisory jurisdiction
(D) the firm's outside law firm

64. The NYSE has a rule that requires a firm to provide a financial statement to a client upon request. The NASD
(A) has a similar rule
(B) members are covered by the NYSE rule
(C) firms can ignore the requirement
(D) complies with the NYSE, although it does not have a similar rule

65. The NASD says that discounts, concessions or allowances on securities transactions
(A) can be granted to any firm in the securities business
(B) shall be granted only to other members of the Association.
(C) shall be expressly forbidden to be given to any individual or firm
(D) are always the responsibility of the member and are not subject to a review

66. Each office of supervisory jurisdiction must
(A) establish, maintain and enforce written procedures as to the supervision of RR's
(B) review the internal written procedures as to the operations functions of the firm
(C) be approved by the NASD
(D) be manned by a general partner or officer holding voting stock.

67. The provisions of the Uniform Practice Code are applied between
(A) members of the NASD
(B) the NASD member firm and the client
(C) the RR of the member firm of the NASD and the client

(D) members of the NASD and non-members.

68. According to the NASD's UPC, written comparisons must be exchanged by parties to a trade

(A) unless the transaction is cleared through the National OTC clearing corporation
(B) in all cases
(C) if the dollar amount of the trade is more than $100
(D) within 7 business days

69. If a client has *not* paid for securities he has bought, his account may be

(A) fined
(B) sold out
(C) marked to the market
(D) bought in

70. The UPC requires that before a trade can be closed out through the buying in procedure,

(A) written notice must be sent one day prior to the execution of the buy in
(B) oral notice must be given one day prior to the execution of the buy in
(C) written notice must be sent 5 business days before the execution of the buy in
(D) written notice of the buy in must be sent at the time the buy in is executed

71. The NASD states that continuing commissions can be paid to an RR who has left a member firm

(A) if a bona fide contract called for such payments
(B) in no cases
(C) of up to 10% of the amount generated in his "old" accounts for 2 years
(D) of up to 50% of the amount generated in his "old" accounts for 1 year.

72. The NASD group which acts as an appellate and review body of complaints is the

(A) SEC
(B) District Business Conduct Committee
(C) Uniform Practice Committee
(D) Board of Governors

73. In a complaint hearing before the NASD, the party(ies) entitled to be represented by counsel are

(A) only the NASD
(B) only the complainant
(C) both the complainant and the NASD
(D) no one; counsel is not permitted

74. The maximum penalty that can be awarded under Summary Complaint Procedures is

(A) a censure and a fine of $500
(B) a censure and a fine of $1,000
(C) only a censure
(D) suspension for 5 business days

75. NASD complaint decisions are subject to review by the SEC

(A) in no cases
(B) upon application by either the NASD or the party concerned
(C) automatically in all cases
(D) only upon application of the person who brought the complaint

CORRECT ANSWERS TO OVER-THE-COUNTER-MARKET AND THE NASD

Number in parenthesis, after answer, identifies number of reference source where information relating to the question and correct answer may be found.

1. A (3)	16. C (3)	31. A (2)	46. D (2)	61. A (2)
2. B (3)	17. B (3)	32. A (2)	47. A (2)	62. C (2)
3. C (3)	18. B (3)	33. D (2)	48. C (2)	63. C (2)
4. B (3)	19. D (2)	34. A (2)	49. D (2)	64. A (2)
5. A (3)	20. D (3)	35. B (2)	50. B (2)	65. B (2)
6. A (3)	21. A (3)	36. C (2)	51. A (2)	66. A (2)
7. B (3)	22. A (3)	37. D (2)	52. A (2)	67. A (2)
8. A (3)	23. A (3)	38. C (2)	53. C (2)	68. A (2)
9. A (3)	24. C (3)	39. A (2)	54. D (2)	69. B (2)
10. B (3)	25. B (3	40. B (2)	55. A (2)	70. A (2)
11. A (3)	26. A	41. D (2)	56. C (2)	71. A (2)
12. A (3)	27. C (3)	42. A (2)	57. A (2)	72. D (2)
13. B (3)	28. B (3)	43. B (2)	58. D (2)	73. C (2)
14. D (3)	29. C (3)	44. A (2)	59. A (2)	74. A (2)
15. C (3)	30. D (3)	45. A (2)	60. D (2)	75. B (2)

LIST OF REFERENCES

1. *New York Stock Exchange Constitution & Rules,* New York Stock Exchange, New York, N. Y.
2. *NASD Manual,* National Association of Securities Dealers, Washington, D. C.
3. *NASD Training Guide,* National Association of Securities Dealers, Washington, D. C.
4. *Fundamentals of the Money Market,* New York Stock Exchange, New York, N. Y.
5. *How to Invest on a Budget — MIP (Monthly Investment Plan),* New York Stock Exchange, New York, N. Y.
6. *The Interpretation of Financial Statements,* Graham & McGolrick — Harper & Row, Publishers, New York, N. Y.
7. *The Stock Market,* Leffler, Farwell — Ronald Press Company, New York, N. Y.
8. *Securities* — Volume 2, Second Edition; *Financial Planning and Mutual Funds,* Kalb, Voorhis & Co., New York, N. Y.
9. *Your Federal Income Tax,* Internal Revenue Service — Production Company, Scarborough, New York.
10. *Manual for Registered Representatives,* Association of Stock Exchange Firms (ASEF), New York, N. Y.
11. *American Stock Exchange Constitution,* American Stock Exchange, New York, N. Y.